STUDENT ACTIVITIES

from the

SENTENCE-COMPOSING TEACHER'S HANDBOOK

STUDENT ACTIVITIES

from the

SENTENCE-COMPOSING TEACHER'S HANDBOOK

by

Don and Jenny Killgallon

Book and ebook design by Booknook.biz

We are grateful for invaluable help from Mark Phillips.

ISBN 979-8376377178

CONTENTS

SENTENCE-COMPOSING METHOD

"Let me live, love, and—
say it well in good sentences."

—Sylvia Plath,
The Unabridged Journals of Sylvia Plath

Sentences unfold one part at a time. The quality of those parts determines the quality of the sentence. The purpose of the activities in this book is to give you an understanding of the sentence-composing method to help you build better sentences by learning, practicing, and using sentence parts authors use as tools to build sentences.

> "You'll never get anywhere with all those damned little short sentences."
>
> —Gregory Clark

To show you how to build better sentences, the sentence-composing method uses these techniques: *chunking, unscrambling, combining, imitating, expanding.* In activities throughout this textbook, you'll use them to build sentences like those of authors, learning, practicing, applying their sentence-composing tools to build better sentences.

CHUNKING

In chunking, a first-step in imitating authors' sentences, you become aware of meaningful versus meaningless divisions within sentences, an awareness needed to imitate an author's sentence, one sentence part—or chunk—at a time.

<u>Directions</u>: What sentence—a or b—imitates the model sentence because its sentence parts (chunks) are the same?

1. <u>Model</u>: I decided / not to open my eyes, / not to get out of bed.
   Rosa Guy, The Friends

   a. Running to catch the bus, I fell and dropped my books.
   b. I wanted only to get the best grade, only to be the best in the class.

2. <u>Model</u>: Soon a glow began / in the dark, / a tiny circle barely red.
   Joseph Krumgold, Onion John

   a. Then a sound came through the night, a small rustle hardly heard.
   b. We planned carefully for the party, wanting it to be a success.

3. <u>Model</u>: Finally, / I sat on a log, / put my gun at my feet, / and waited.
   Phyllis Reynolds Naylor, Shiloh

   a. Wondering what to do next, I just leaned against the wall and stared into the sky.
   b. Occasionally, I walked down the path, carried my camera around my neck, and looked.

4. <u>Model</u>: His face / was bloody, / his shirt torn / and bloody down the front.

Hal Borland, *When the Legends Die*

    a. The day was perfect, the sky blue and brilliant in the heavens.
    b. His sister married someone they didn't know, a stranger to the family.

5. <u>Model</u>: Big, rough teenagers / jostled through the crowd, / their rolled sleeves high enough / to show off blue and red tattoos.

Robert Lipsyte, *The Contender*

    a. Silent, silver fish moved through the tank, their shiny bodies heavy enough to suggest larger and more dangerous predators.
    b. An old, large man reached for the available chair and sat down, huffing and puffing, before I could get there to assist him.

Remember this: When you imitate an author's sentence, do one chunk (sentence part) at a time. That way, imitating the sentence is much easier.

UNSCRAMBLING

Unscrambling sentence parts of an author's sentence helps you see the connection between meaning and structure. You unscramble a list of sentence parts from an imitation sentence to match the sentence parts of a model sentence.

Directions: Unscramble the sentence parts to imitate the model. Then write your own imitation of the model about something you know, something you've experienced, or something you've seen in the media.

1. Model: When I awoke, there were snowflakes on my eyes.
   Charles Portis, *True Grit*

   a. in the sky
   b. there was a rainbow
   c. after the rain stopped

2. Model: Drawn by the scent of fish, the wild dogs sat on the hill, barking and growling at each other.
   Scott O'Dell, *Island of Blue Dolphins*

   a. yelping and squealing with delight
   b. covered with mud from the yard
   c. the frisky puppy rolled on the carpet

3. Model: Then she swung the switch five more times and, discovering Little Man had no intention of crying, ordered him up.
   Mildred D. Taylor, *Roll of Thunder, Hear My Cry*

    a.   one more time and

    b.   shut the case down

    c.   then he checked the crime scene

    d.   finding the suspect had been telling the truth

4.   <u>Model</u>: The girls of her class nearly fought to hang out around her, to walk away with her, to beam flatteringly, to be her special friend.

                                        Katherine Mansfield, "The Doll's House"

    a.   really tried to make his best effort with them

    b.   to keep up with them

    c.   to be his absolute best

    d.   the boy of smallest size

    e.   to work tirelessly

COMBINING

Using content from a list of sentences, you create the model's structure, working one sentence part at a time.

<u>Directions</u>: Combine the sentences to create a sentence with the same sentence parts as the model. Then write your own imitation of the model about something you know, something you've experienced, or something you've seen in the media.

1. <u>Model</u>: The children, shouting and screaming, came charging back into their homeroom.

   Rosa Guy, *The Friends*

   a. The ponies came bolting out of their stalls.
   b. The ponies were pawing.
   c. Also, the ponies were neighing.

2. <u>Model</u>: As Seabiscuit broke from the gate, he was immediately bashed inward by Count Atlas, a hopeless long shot emerging from the stall on Seabiscuit's right.

   Hillenbrand, *Seabiscuit: An American Legend*

   a. Something happened as the car backed out of the space.
   b. What happened was that it was suddenly hit sideways.
   c. The hit was by an oncoming truck.
   d. The truck was a delivery pickup.
   e. The pickup was coming from the alley behind the market.

3.   <u>Model</u>: A light kindled in the sky, a blaze of yellow fire behind dark barriers.

J. R. R. Tolkien, *The Lord of the Rings*

    a.   A noise erupted.
    b.   The noise erupted from the forest.
    c.   The noise was a screech.
    d.   The screech was of angry ravens.
    e.   The ravens were in decayed trees.

4.   <u>Model</u>: He knew the bears would soon be leaving their winter dens, to travel, to claim their old ranges, to challenge intruders, and to fight their fearful battles among themselves.

Hal Borland, *When the Legends Die*

    a.   She knew something about the students.
    b.   She knew they would soon be entering their new classrooms.
    c.   The students would be entering the classrooms to learn.
    d.   They would also be entering them to take new courses.
    e.   They would also be entering them to make new friends.
    f.   In addition, they would be entering them to discover their identities as young adults.

EXPANDING

Given a model sentence with a sentence part deleted at the caret mark (^), you write something to add at that place in the model sentence.

Example

Model Sentence

On the screen, Rebecca's face appeared, ^ , and she saw that she really had been having a wonderful time.

Anne Tyler, Back When We Were Grownups

Expanded with Different Kinds of Additions:

1. On the screen, Rebecca's face appeared, **softening from her grimace**, and she saw that she really had been having a wonderful time.

2. On the screen, Rebecca's face appeared, **with a slow, gentle smile**, and she saw that she really had been having a wonderful time.

3. On the screen, Rebecca's face appeared, **which revealed a loosening pout**, and she saw that she really had been having a wonderful time.

Original Sentence: On the screen, Rebecca's face appeared, **merry and open and sunlit**, and she saw that she really had been having a wonderful time.

Directions: At the caret (^) add a sentence part beginning with the word provided.

1. The dragon came crashing out of the underbrush, **with** ^ .

2. The dragon came crashing out of the underbrush, **threatening** ^ .

3. The dragon came crashing out of the underbrush, **its** ^ .

IMITATING

Sentences have content and structure. When you imitate a model sentence, you imitate only the *structure* of an author's model sentence but create your own content. For example, if the model is about fishing, write about walking, racing, studying, dancing, singing, eating, or any other activity—but *not* fishing. In imitating a model sentence, you partner with an author, using the author's structure but your topic.

Below, slash marks divide the model sentence into chunks (sentence parts) for you to imitate one chunk at a time. A sample imitation illustrates the similarity in sentence parts between the two sentences—the model and the sample imitation. Notice that each sample imitation uses only the author's structure, but new content.

Directions: Choose one of the models and then write an imitation built like the model but about new content.

1. Model: He was white and shaking, / his mouth opening and shutting / without words.

   Leslie Morris, "Three Shots for Charlie Beston"

   Sample Imitation: Darlene was happy and smiling, / her voice lovely and soothing / like music.

2. Model: Now, / leaning his head out of the window / of the pickup, / he thought he would die / of thirst.

   Katherine Paterson, *Park's Quest*

   Sample Imitation: Then, / visiting the market outside of the farm / near the pasture, Waldo believed he would live / on vegetables.

3. <u>Model</u>: Hobbling on one foot, / Wanda opened the closet door / and turned / on the light.

Betsy Byars, The Summer of the Swans

<u>Sample Imitation</u>: Knocking over the kitchen fence, / the puppy reached the food dish / and drank / from the bowl.

4. <u>Model</u>: Propped on her elbows / with her chin in her fists, / she stared at the black wolf, / trying to catch his eye.

Jean Craighead George, Julie of the Wolves

<u>Sample Imitation</u>: Concerned about its safety, / with his hands on its shoulders, / Dad walked with the unsteady toddler, / wanting to prevent its fall.

5. <u>Model</u>: To avoid embarrassment / and to make the job easier, / all students / quickly learned / certain interviewing tricks.

Michael Crichton, Travels

<u>Sample Imitation</u>: To add comfort / and to make the bed warmer, / most campers / smartly added / more warm blankets.

The sentence-composing activities in this chapter—*chunking, unscrambling, combining, expanding, imitating*—provide an effective way to learn sentence-building tools authors use to build their sentences.

All activities use imitation. Imitating authors' sentences is the foundation of the sentence-composing method for building better sentences.

> "Stylistic imitation is a perfectly honorable way to get started as a writer and impossible to avoid, really; some sort of imitation marks each new stage of a writer's development...."
>
> —Stephen King, *On Writing*

Within you and everyone is an inborn capacity to learn by imitating others—in talking or walking, in choosing clothes or grooming hair, in hitting a tennis ball or throwing a baseball, in learning just about anything. To learn almost anything, you need someone who knows how to do it, a model to imitate. In the sentence-composing method, your teacher is an author, an expert in building sentences, a model to imitate to build better sentences.

Immersing you in a sentence-rich environment, sentence-composing activities in this book teach you through imitation how to build strong sentences like those of authors. Breaking a model sentence by an author into sentence parts (chunks), then imitating one chunk at a time, makes imitating a model sentence simple. *Remember this*: the best way to eat an elephant is one bite at a time.

In the models and imitations below, notice how the sentence parts (chunks) are built the same way.

1a. <u>Model</u>: Uno stepped up / to the makeshift home plate, / an overturned metal trash can lid, / and waved a duct-taped bat / through the strike zone.
Matt de la Pena, Mexican WhiteBoy (adapted)

1b. <u>Imitation</u>: Benny went out / to the dilapidated storage shed, / a home-made plywood box-like thing, / and threw a 50-foot hose / onto the pile.

2a. <u>Model</u>: Then / the face appeared / before her, / floating in the darkness, / a horrible face / from a nightmare.
Stephen King, The Dead Zone

2b. <u>Imitation</u>: Now / the memory returned / to him, / awakening in the night, / a sudden flashback / to the accident.

3a. <u>Model</u>: The country / hailed Althea Gibson, / the tennis player / who was the first black female / to win the U.S. Women's Singles.
Maya Angelou, The Heart of a Woman

3b. <u>Imitation</u>: The children / enjoyed Ronald McDonald, / the colorful clown / who was the chosen character / to represent the worldwide food chain.

4a. <u>Model</u>: Full of fear, / the rabbit paddled and struggled, / got his head up and took a breath, / scrabbled his claws against rough bricks under water / and lost them again / as he was dragged on.
Richard Adams, Watership Down

4b. <u>Imitation</u>: Ready to fight, / the boxer bobbed and swayed, / put his fists up and took a swing, / pushed his glove toward the exposed jaw of his opponent in a jab / and hit him again / as his opponent was falling down.

5a. <u>Model</u>: In hunting season, / all kinds of small game / turn up in dumpsters, / some of it, / sadly, / not entirely dead.

Lars Eighner, "On Dumpster Diving"

5b. <u>Imitation</u>: On summer beaches, / all sorts of body shapes / lie down on towels, / many of them, / unfortunately, / not particularly attractive.

If your imitation sentence is exact, fine; if approximate, fine, too. In both, you are using new sentence patterns, which is the goal of the entire sentence-composing method for building better sentences.

When you imitate sentences of authors, you resemble an art student creating a new painting that mirrors Picasso's style, a music student composing a new concerto reflecting Mozart's style. In any endeavor, artistic or otherwise—in building a skyscraper or in building a sentence, a model is both an end-point and a starting-point. In imitating model sentences, you borrow something (sentence structure) and contribute something (sentence content), through a merger of imitation and creation.

Famous author Robert Louis Stevenson claimed that "imitation is the only way to learn to write." He advocated imitating many authors, experimenting with their styles. As a result of new awareness of possibilities in style through imitating many styles, you can develop your own unique style. In short, you imitate in order to innovate.

> "Imitation is in fact part of the writing process. For writers imitate other writers, just as surely as painters imitate other painters, violinists imitate other violinists, golfers imitate other golfers. It's one of the ways beginners learn how it's done."
>
> —Donna Gorrell, "Freedom to Write—through Imitation"

A baby learns to speak sentences by imitating the sentences of people who know how to talk. You can learn to write sentences by imitating the sentences of authors who know how to write. In this book, you'll have lots of practice doing exactly that, learning to build stronger sentences, ones like those of an author. The rest of this book shows you how.

SENTENCE-COMPOSING TOOLBOX

"Good writing consists of filling your toolbox with the right instruments."

—Stephen King, *On Writing*

Earlier, you learned how sentences unfold one part at a time, and that they determine how a sentence is built, well or poorly.

Now you'll learn how to build *good* sentence parts—the kind authors use as tools to build their sentences so your sentences are well built.

How authors build sentences differs from how most people build sentences. The difference is that authors build theirs with sentence-composing tools most people don't have or don't use in the same way.

> "The sentence is the greatest invention of civilization."
>
> —John Banville, novelist and screenwriter

The "Sentence-Composing Toolbox" contains powerful sentence-composing tools used frequently by authors, infrequently by students, each tool taught through authors' sentences using the tool. Here are the tools you'll learn.

SENTENCE-COMPOSING TOOLBOX

MULTIPLE SUBJECT   Page 21

<u>Example</u>: **The sun bugs, the flies, the dragonflies, the wasps, the hornets** went home.

John Steinbeck, *Cannery Row*

MULTIPLE PREDICATE   Page 25

<u>Example</u>: The cloaked figure **reached the unicorn, lowered its head over the wound in the animal's side**, and **began to drink its blood**.

J. K. Rowling, *Harry Potter*

OPENING ADJECTIVE   Page 33

<u>Example</u>: **High in the branches**, he had a good view of the forest.

Michael Crichton, *Jurassic Park*

DELAYED ADJECTIVE   Page 39

<u>Example</u>: His teeth, **strong enough to shatter walnuts**, were still intact.

Truman Capote, *In Cold Blood*

OPENING ADVERB   Page 45

<u>Example</u>: **Slowly, methodically, miserably**, she ate the jellied bread.

Toni Morrison, *Beloved*

DELAYED ADVERB   **Page 51**

<u>Example</u>: When he saw that I was looking at him, he closed his eyes, **sleepily**, **angelically**, then stuck out his tongue.

J. D. Salinger, "For Esmé—with Love and Squalor"

ABSOLUTE PHRASE   **Page 55**

<u>Example</u>: Boo Radley had been leaning against the wall when I came into the room, **his arms folded across his chest**.

Harper Lee, *To Kill a Mockingbird*

APPOSITIVE PHRASE   **Page 61**

<u>Example</u>: The country hailed Althea Gibson, **the tennis player who was the first black female to win the U.S. Women's Singles**.

Maya Angelou, *The Heart of a Woman*

PARTICIPLE PHRASE   **Page 67**

<u>Example</u>: Flies buzzed in through the door, **landing on the open watermelons and the sweet corn**.

Robert Lipsyte, *The Contender*

PREPOSITIONAL PHRASE   **Page 75**

<u>Example</u>: **On the whole enormous prairie**, there was no sign that any other human being had ever been there.

Laura Ingalls *Wilder, Little House on the Prairie*

ADJECTIVE CLAUSE **Page 81**

<u>Example</u>: The sheep, **which had moved lightly away as he had come into the pasture**, turned now to stare at him.

Katherine Paterson, *Park's Quest*

ADVERB CLAUSE **Page 89**

<u>Example</u>: With a gentle forefinger, he stroked the turtle's throat **until the horny-toad relaxed, until its eyes closed** and **until it lay asleep**.

John Steinbeck, *The Red Pony*

You'll learn, practice, and apply each sentence-composing tool through varied activities: chunking, unscrambling, combining, expanding, and imitating.

Along the way, you'll build a sentence-composing toolbox filled with power tools to use whenever and whatever you write, with sentences like those of authors.

MULTIPLE SUBJECT

A multiple subject is several topics (persons, places, or things) commented upon by the predicate.

Examples

1. **Mrs. Salt** and **Mrs. Teavee** were getting very out of breath.
   Roald Dahl, *Charlie and the Chocolate Factory*

2. **The very old man** and **the very old woman** ran into the house as fast as they could.
   Wanda Gag, "Millions of Cats"

3. **A strong current** and **a high wind** carried the peach so quickly away from the shore that already the land was out of sight.
   Roald Dahl, *James and the Giant Peach*

4. **Mr. Fox** and **Mrs. Fox** and **their four Small Foxes** lived in the hole.
   Roald Dahl, *Fantastic Mr. Fox* (adapted)

5. **The clothesline**, **the penguin**, **Mr. Popper** and **the tripod** were all tangled up.
   Richard and Florence Atwater, *Mr. Popper's Penguins*

ACTIVITY 1—MULTIPLE SUBJECT

Directions: Combine the sentence parts to imitate the model.

1. Model: Smoke and flames were pouring out of the blackened spaces where the windows had been.

   Franklin W. Dixon, *The Secret of the Old Mill*

   a. There were **stores** and **restaurants**.
   b. They were going up on the site.
   c. The site was where my school had been.

2. Model: **Four days**, **eight days**, **twelve days** passed, and he was invited to teas, to suppers, to lunches.

   Ray Bradbury, *Dandelion Wine*

   a. The **many mornings** came.
   b. The **many afternoons** also came.
   c. The **many nights** also came.
   d. And she was tormented by memories.
   e. She was tormented by suspicions.
   f. She was tormented by betrayals.

3. Model: Next moment **the luggage**, **the seat**, **the platform**, and **the station** had completely vanished.

   C. S. Lewis, *The Chronicles of Narnia: Prince Caspian*

   a. That time **the students** did something.
   b. And **their parents** did something.
   c. And **their grandparents** did something.
   d. And **their teachers** did something.
   e. They had loudly applauded.

ACTIVITY 2—MULTIPLE SUBJECT

Directions: The model and the sample imitation are built with similar sentence parts. Write an imitation, one sentence part at a time, about something you know, something you've experienced, or something you've seen in the media.

1. Model: **Stars, comets, planets** flashed across the sky.
   > Madeleine L'Engle, *A Wrinkle in Time*

   Sample Imitation: **Bottles, cans, boxes** poured into the recyclables.

2. Model: **Dad** and **some of his Air Force buddies** were on a cliff of the canyon, trying to work up the nerve to dive into the lake forty feet below.
   > Jeannette Walls, *The Glass Castle*

   Sample Imitation: **Susan** and **many of her cheering friends** were on the field of the high school, starting to show off their cheers to compete with the other team's performance.

3. Model: **The great square jaws and head, his muscular neck and broad chest** showed his bulldog blood.
   > William Armstrong, *Sounder*

   Sample Imitation: **A large mole and scar, his bald head and bushy eyebrows** matched the criminal's profile.

ACTIVITY 3—EXPANDING

Directions: Study the examples of multiple subjects, and then in the basic paragraph add subjects at the carets (^).

Examples of Multiple Subjects

1. **The sun bugs, the flies, the dragonflies, the wasps, the hornets** went home.
   > John Steinbeck, *Cannery Row*

2. **Letters, computer printouts, forbiddingly thick bound documents** covered the mayor's desk, a sturdy oak table.
   > Ray Bradbury, *The Illustrated Man*

3. **The effort of moving the piano the day before, a sleepless night, weeks of worry and unbalanced diet, the cares of his parish** combined to make him feel hardly adequate to the new day's work.
   > John Hersey, *Hiroshima*

BASIC PARAGRAPH

1. The ^ and a ^ at a crime scene found an important clue to the crime. 2. It was a piece of glass from a broken window. 3. That clue, ^ , and ^ could make the case. 4. It was just the evidence he needed. 5. Some ^ and a ^ said they weren't anywhere near the crime scene.

NUGGETS FOR WRITING

<u>Directions</u>: Choose A PARTY or A PET or A TOY to create a five-sentence paragraph with **multiple subjects**. Underline each multiple subject.

- ✓ Read the sample paragraph below.
- ✓ Revise your paragraph so well it could be published.
- ✓ Give your paragraph a creative title understandable only after reading.

SAMPLE PARAGRAPH for A PET

"DIVIDE AND CONQUER"

1. <u>Ridley, Louie, and Kiwi</u>, nicknamed the Beagle Boys, assembled at the back door, impatient, waiting for Barbara to let them in. 2. In their dishes, <u>the dog food and leftovers from last night's dinner</u> were in plain sight of the threesome. 3. Ridley, the most insistent, began howling. 4. <u>Barbara, John, and Mer</u> went outside, each taking one dog to bring in. 5. Of the same mind, they had learned to divide and conquer.

MULTIPLE PREDICATE

A multiple predicate is when several comments within the sentence refer to the subject.

Examples

1. <u>The two girls</u> **groped their way among the other sleepers and crept out of the tent**.

    C. S. Lewis, *The Lion, the Witch and the Wardrobe*

2. <u>Water</u> **dripped off her matted hair and ran in icy trickles down her back**.

    Elizabeth George Speare, *The Witch of Blackbird Pond*

3. <u>She</u> **took a deep breath, then smiled, and patted the rabbit on its head**.

    Lois Lenski, *Strawberry Girl*

4. <u>He</u> **became conscious of the weight of clothes, kicked his shoes off fiercely, and ripped off each stocking with its elastic garter in a single movement**.

    William Golding, *Lord of the Flies*

5. <u>The wasp</u> **went into a hole in the ground, came out, flew away, and came back**.

    Jean Craighead George, *The Fire Bug Connection*

ACTIVITY 1—COMBINING

<u>Directions</u>: Combine the sentence parts to imitate the model.

1. <u>Model</u>: He laughed, waved his hand, started the engine.
    Phyllis Reynolds Naylor, Shiloh (adapted)

    a. Gerty did three things.
    b. She coughed.
    c. grabbed the water.
    d. took a drink.

2. <u>Model</u>: The cloaked figure reached the unicorn, lowered its head over the wound in the animal's side, and began to drink its blood.
    J. K. Rowling, Harry Potter

    a. The curious toddler did several things.
    b. He saw the puppy.
    c. He moved his body over the carpet to the puppy's cage.
    d. And the toddler reached to pet its fur.

3. <u>Model</u>: When the headaches struck, the general went to his room, undressed, turned off the light, locked the door, and didn't come out until the pain subsided.
    Khaled Hosseini, The Kite Runner

    a. Something happened when the rain eased.
    b. What happened was the children headed for the park.
    c. They played in the puddles.
    d. They romped.
    e. They climbed a tree.
    f. They chased a squirrel.
    g. And they didn't think about the weather until the thunder clapped.

ACTIVITY 2—IMITATING

Directions: The model and the sample imitation are built with similar sentence parts. Write an imitation, one sentence part at a time, about something you know, something you've experienced, or something you've seen in the media.

1. Model: The snake **took one look at all of us**, **turned around**, and **wriggled away toward the hills**.

   Michael Crichton, *Travels*

   Sample Imitation: The child **heard one shout from all of them, looked anxiously, and ran quickly to his parents**.

2. Model: I **climbed trees, played hopscotch, jumped rope, skated, swam, rode my bicycle, sailed**.

   Nancy Mairs, *Plaintext*

   Sample Imitation: Sammy **read books, called friends, walked trails, exercised, ate, listened to music, relaxed**.

3. Model: Mack **awakened, started up, stretched, staggered to the pool, washed his face with cupped hands, hacked, spat, washed out his mouth, tightened his belt, scratched his legs, combed his wet hair with his fingers, drank from the jug, belched**, and **sat down by the fire**.

   John Steinbeck, *Cannery Row*

   Sample Imitation: Jackson **stood, warmed up, walked, sat on a bench, resumed his exercise on the forest trail, paused, sat, took out his camera, aimed the camera, adjusted the lens, shot the clouds within the blue sky, aimed at a fox, steadied**, and **focused slowly on the animal**.

ACTIVITY 3—EXPANDING

Directions: Study the examples below of multiple predicates, and then in the basic paragraph add predicates at the carets (^).

Examples of Multiple Predicates

1.   Crookshanks **skidded to a halt, crouched low on his bandy legs**, and **started making furious swipes beneath it with his front paw.**

J. K. Rowling, Harry Potter

2.   The boy **put Sounder's tin under the porch, closed the door, pushed the night latch, sat down behind the stove**, and **began to eat his supper.**

William H. Armstrong, Sounder

3.   Mrs. Jones **stopped, jerked him around in front of her, put a half nelson about his neck**, and **continued to drag him up the street.**

Langston Hughes, "Thank You, M'am"

BASIC PARAGRAPH

1. The skaters appeared on the ice, ^ . 2. He held her in his arms, ^ . 3. Their music was a classical piece. 4. They performed lifts, ^ . 5. The audience liked them.

NUGGETS FOR WRITING

<u>Directions</u>: Choose AN ACCIDENT or A FAILURE or A MYSTERY to create a five-sentence paragraph with **multiple predicates**. Underline each multiple predicate.

- ✓ Read the sample paragraph below.
- ✓ Revise your paragraph so well it could be published.
- ✓ Give your paragraph a creative title understandable only after reading.

SAMPLE PARAGRAPH for A MYSTERY

"THIN AIR"

1. Responding to the 911 call, Michael, the first responder, <u>scanned the room, noticed the unmade bed, wondered where its occupant had gone</u>. 2. He <u>went to the bed, felt the warmth of the sheets, and knew that he had just missed someone</u>. 3. Perplexed, he <u>wondered where the person had gone, thought about what to do next, searched the other rooms, hoped the occupant was not in trouble and not making trouble</u>. 4. Uncertain, he <u>raised his voice, hoped for a response, and waited for someone to respond and appear</u>. 5. Still alone when no one responded, Michael <u>gave up, went outside back to the ambulance, called his dispatcher to explain what happened, and drove off</u>.

"A sentence is itself a story, with a beginning, a middle, and an end.
Something happens in a sentence.
Without subjects, there are no heroes or villains.
Without verbs, there is no action.
Without objects, nothing is moved, changed, destroyed, or created."

—Linton Weeks, "The Fate of the Sentence"

SENTENCE-COMPOSING TOOLBOX

A subject and its predicate are the foundation of a sentence. What follows are sentence parts that authors use as tools to add detail and texture to that foundation.

This chapter, the most important part of this book, teaches you power tools to learn, practice, and use to build stronger, often much stronger, sentences. Each tool is defined, illustrated in authors' sentences, practiced, and applied to your writing.

> "Good writing consists of filling your toolbox
> with the right instruments."
>
> —Stephen King, *On Writing*

MULTIPLE SUBJECT Page 21

Example: **The sun bugs, the flies, the dragonflies, the wasps, the hornets** went home.

John Steinbeck, *Cannery Row*

MULTIPLE PREDICATE Page 25

Example: The cloaked figure **reached the unicorn, lowered its head over the wound in the animal's side,** and **began to drink its blood.**

J. K. Rowling, *Harry Potter*

OPENING ADJECTIVE Page 33

Example: **High in the branches,** he had a good view of the forest.

Michael Crichton, *Jurassic Park*

DELAYED ADJECTIVE   **Page 39**

Example: His teeth, **strong enough to shatter walnuts**, were still intact.

Truman Capote, In Cold Blood

OPENING ADVERB   **Page 45**

Example: **Slowly**, **methodically**, **miserably**, she ate the jellied bread.

Toni Morrison, Beloved

DELAYED ADVERB   **Page 51**

Example: When he saw that I was looking at him, he closed his eyes, **sleepily**, **angelically**, then stuck out his tongue.

J. D. Salinger, "For Esmé—with Love and Squalor"

ABSOLUTE PHRASE   **Page 55**

Example: Boo Radley had been leaning against the wall when I came into the room, **his arms folded across his chest**.

Harper Lee, To Kill a Mockingbird

APPOSITIVE PHRASE   **Page 61**

Example: The country hailed Althea Gibson, **the tennis player who was the first black female to win the U.S. Women's Singles**.

Maya Angelou, The Heart of a Woman.

PARTICIPLE PHRASE   **Page 67**

Example: Flies buzzed in through the door, **landing on the open watermelons and the sweet corn**.

Robert Lipsyte, The Contender

PREPOSITIONAL PHRASE   Page 75

<u>Example</u>: **On the whole enormous prairie**, there was no sign that any other human being had ever been there.

Laura Ingalls *Wilder, Little House on the Prairie*

ADJECTIVE CLAUSE   Page 81

<u>Example</u>: The sheep, **which had moved lightly away as he had come into the pasture**, turned now to stare at him.

Katherine Paterson, *Park's Quest*

ADVERB CLAUSE   Page 89

<u>Example</u>: With a gentle forefinger, he stroked the turtle's throat **until the horny-toad relaxed, until its eyes closed** and **until it lay asleep**.

John Steinbeck, *The Red Pony*

OPENING ADJECTIVE

An adjective describes a person, place, or thing. Authors sometimes use one or more adjectives to open a sentence. The adjective may be a single adjective, multiple adjectives, or an adjective phrase. A comma follows an opening adjective.

Single Opening Adjective

a. **Rigid**, I began climbing the rungs, slightly reassured by having Finny right behind me. (*Rigid* describes *I*.)

   John Knowles, *A Separate Peace*

b. **Hungry**, Thomas ate two portions of meat, nothing else. (*Hungry* describes *Thomas*.)

   Hal Borland, *When the Legends Die*

c. **Curious**, he tore the end off the envelope, which was no easy task with fingers beginning to stiffen from the cold. (*Curious* describes *he*.)

   William P. Young, *The Shack*

Multiple Opening Adjectives

d. **Slow** and **unkempt**, he looked as if he had slept in his clothes, and in fact he often did, after a marathon programming session. (*Slow* and *unkempt* describe *he*.)

   Michael Crichton, *Prey*

e. **Hungry** and **afraid**, James stood alone out in the open, wondering what to do. (*Hungry* and *afraid* describe *James.*)

> Roald Dahl, *James and the Giant Peach*

f. **Fresh**, **vital**, **lively**, spring enveloped all of us. (*Fresh, vital, lively* describe *spring.*)

> Mildred D. Taylor, *Roll of Thunder, Hear My Cry* (adapted)

Opening Adjective Phrase

g. **Certain of herself**, Carlotta flung herself into her part without restraint or modesty. (*Certain of herself* describes *Carlotta.*)

> Gaston Leroux, *The Phantom of the Opera*

h. **Numb of all feeling**, he still clung to life. (*Numb of all feeling* describes *he.*)

> Armstrong Perry, *Call It Courage*

i. **Blind from birth**, Beatrice has passed all nineteen years of her life so far pretty much limited to the house. (*Blind from birth* describes Beatrice.)

> Fannie Flagg, *Standing in the Rainbow*

ACTIVITY 1–UNSCRAMBLING

<u>Directions</u>: Unscramble the sentence parts to imitate the model.

1. <u>Model</u>: **Desperate**, Frodo drew his own sword, and it seemed to him that it flickered red, as if it were a firebrand.

> J. R. R. Tolkien, *The Lord of the Rings*

a. that the board bounced repeatedly
b. and it appeared to him
c. as if it were a trampoline
d. **nervous**
e. Jackson walked the diving board

2. <u>Model</u>: **Cold** and **wet** and **dirty**, I realized that I was alone for the first time in months.

Donohue, Keith, The Stolen Child

    a.   the actress knew
    b.   by the entire audience on their feet
    c.   lucky and happy and sweet
    d.   that she was loved

3. <u>Model</u>: **High in the branches**, he had a good view of the forest.

Michael Crichton, Jurassic Park

    a.   on the racket
    b.   Jackson
    c.   got a firm grip
    d.   tight on its handle

ACTIVITY 2–IMITATING

<u>Directions</u>: The model and the sample imitation are built with similar sentence parts. Write an imitation, one sentence part at a time, about something you know, something you've experienced, or something you've seen in the media

1. <u>Model</u>: **Unsteady**, / he carefully turned around, / trying to hold on to some sense of sanity.

William P. Young, The Shack

<u>Sample Imitation</u>: **Nervous**, / Barry fearfully looked down, / hoping to grab on to a branch of the tree.

2. <u>Model</u>: **Bloodthirsty** and **brutal**, / the giants / brought themselves to the point of extinction / by warring amongst themselves / during the last century.

J. K. Rowling, Harry Potter

<u>Sample Imitation</u>: **Exciting** and **entertaining**, / the singer / worked herself to the edge of exhaustion / by straining with her voice / in the previous songs.

3. <u>Model</u>: **Immune / to the assorted nauseas / of space travel**, Scott moved / to take her place / at the crystal viewport.

Lois McMaster Bujold, Falling Free

<u>Sample Imitation</u>: **Curious / about the various colors / of oil paint**, Sandra wanted / to paint the scene / with her artistic best.

ACTIVITY 3–EXPANDING

<u>Directions</u>: Study the examples of opening adjectives, and then in the basic paragraph add a <u>single opening adjective, multiple opening adjectives, or an opening adjective phrase</u> at the carets (^).

Examples of Opening Adjectives

1. <u>single</u>: **Comfortable**, I lay on my back and waited for sleep, and while waiting I thought of Dill. (*Comfortable* describes *I*.)

Harper Lee, To Kill a Mockingbird

2. <u>multiple</u>: **Stiff, cold,** and **bruised**, they seized the ends of their trunks and began dragging them up the grassy slope toward the great oak front doors. (*Stiff, cold,* and *bruised* describe *they*.)

J. K. Rowling, Harry Potter

3. <u>phrase</u>: **Able to move now,** he rocked his own body back and forth, breathing deeply to release the remembered pain. (*Able to move now* describes *he*.)

Lois Lowry, The Giver

BASIC PARAGRAPH

1. ^, Talia found a nice shell at the beach. 2. ^ , she brought it home and cleaned it. 3. Then it was shiny and bright. 4. ^ , it looked like a jewel. 5. It didn't look like something found on the beach.

NUGGETS FOR WRITING

<u>Directions</u>: Choose A SUCCESS STORY or A FUN TIME or A MEMORABLE EXPERIENCE to create a five-sentence paragraph with a variety of **opening adjectives**. Underline each opening adjective.

- ✓ Read the sample paragraph below.
- ✓ Revise your paragraph so well it could be published.
- ✓ Give your paragraph a creative title understandable only after reading.

SAMPLE PARAGRAPH for A SUCCESS STORY

"JELLING"

1. <u>Alone</u>, the captain of the volleyball team, looking at a video of their last game, thought about what she hoped for, a win at the finals. 2. <u>Together after many false starts</u>, her team was finally beginning to jell, working as a unit. 3. <u>Intent on building team spirit</u>, they were winning game after game, building confidence as they built skill. 4. <u>Uncertain but hopeful</u>, she envisioned a championship game because they had made it to the play-offs. 5. <u>Resolute in spirit</u>, they could make this victory happen.

DELAYED ADJECTIVE

A delayed adjective comes after the word it describes. The adjective may be a single adjective, multiple adjectives, or an adjective phrase. Commas punctuate delayed adjectives: one comma if the delayed adjective ends the sentence, two commas if it occurs earlier.

Single Delayed Adjective

    a.   I was at peace, **happy**. (*Happy* describes *I*.)

Christy Brown, My Left Foot

    b.   He paused in his humming song, and the bear's ears stiffened, **alert**. (*Alert* describes *the bear's ears*.)

Hal Borland, When the Legends Die

    c.   Old Man Matthews, **stocky**, came first, with his two sons. (*Stocky* describes *Old Man Matthews*.)

Gina Berriault, "The Stone Boy"

Multiple Delayed Adjectives

    d.   Our father was younger than the landlord, **leaner**, **stronger**, and **bigger**. (*Leaner, stronger, bigger* describe *our father*.)

James Baldwin, Tell Me How Long the Train's Been Gone

e. This is a snail shell, **round, full**, and **glossy**. (*Round, full, glossy* describe *snail shell*.)

Anne Morrow Lindbergh, Gift from the Sea

f. The first thing Rainsford's eyes discerned was the largest man Rainsford had ever seen, a gigantic creature, **fierce, strong**, but **gentle**. (*Fierce, strong, gentle* describe *a gigantic creature*.)

Richard Connell, "The Most Dangerous Game" (adapted)

Delayed Adjective Phrase

g. Gatsby, **vivid with excitement,** sprang to his feet. (*Vivid with excitement* describes *Gatsby*.)

F. Scott Fitzgerald, The Great Gatsby (adapted)

h. Jonas felt more and more certain that the destination lay ahead of him, **near now in the night that was approaching**. (*Near now in the night that was approaching* describes *the destination*.)

Lois Lowry, The Giver

i. The great white bed, **huge as a prairie, built up with layer upon solid layer of mattress, blanket, and quilt**, almost filled the little shadowy room in which it stood. (*Huge as a prairie, built up with layer upon solid layer of mattress, blanket, and quilt* describes *the great white bed*.)

Joan Aiken, "Searching for Summer"

ACTIVITY 1—COMBINING

<u>Directions</u>: Combine the sentences to imitate the model.

1. <u>Model</u>: First snow came, six inches of it in the night, **fluffy**.

Hal Borland, When the Legends Die

    a. Soon grass appeared.
    b. There was loads of it.
    c. It was in the yard.
    d. The grass was **thick**.

2. <u>Model</u>: There is a spider in the bathroom of uncertain lineage, **bulbous at the abdomen**.

Annie Dillard, "Death of a Moth"

    a. There is a hallway.
    b. It is in the attic.
    c. It is in a dim light.
    d. It is **spooky along the way**.

3. <u>Model</u>: At one point a raven, **black** and **lustrous**, came flapping out from a bush and flew alongside us, his hoarse cackle weird and hollow.

Bill and Vera Cleaver, *Where the Lilies Bloom*

    a. Amid the crowd the beggar started coming toward us from the alley.
    b. The beggar was **dirty** and **stark**.
    c. And the beggar inched toward my dad.
    d. The beggar's pathetic plea was urgent and sad.

ACTIVITY 2—IMITATING

<u>Directions</u>: The model and the sample imitation are built with similar sentence parts. Write an imitation, one sentence part at a time, about something you know, something you've experienced, or something you've seen in the media.

1. <u>Model</u>: The great white bed, **huge as a prairie**, almost filled the little shadowy room in which it stood.

Joan Aiken, "Searching for Summer" (adapted)

    <u>Sample Imitation</u>: The small inviting room, **cozy as a quilt**, always had soft, comfortable chairs in which guests rested.

2. <u>Model</u>: His eyebrows, **thick** and **black**, had kept their old defiant arch.

Roya Hakakian, *Journey from the Land of No*

    <u>Sample Imitation</u>: Pam's braids, **long** and **blonde**, had seen some better days.

3. Model: After she kicked Uncle Jack out of the house, she looked even better, **happier, looser, janglier, jaunty.**

Garrison Keillor, Pontoon

Sample Imitation: When Albert won valedictorian of his class, he seemed almost better, **kinder, friendlier, wittier, charming**.

4. Model: His teeth, **strong enough to shatter walnuts**, were still intact.

Truman Capote, In Cold Blood

Sample Imitation: His eyes, **alert enough to spot danger**, were always watching.

ACTIVITY 3—EXPANDING

Directions: Study the examples of delayed adjectives, and then in the basic paragraph add delayed adjectives at the carets (^).

Examples of Delayed Adjectives

1. single adjective: The bear's ears stiffened, **alert**. (*Alert* describes the bear's ears.)

Hal Borland, When the Legends Die

2. multiple adjectives: The sun hung high in the blue sky, **warm, hot, yellow, and fine**. (*Warm, hot, yellow, fine* describe the sun.)

Ray Bradbury, The Illustrated Man

3. adjective phrase: In the distance, Kiser Pease, **high on his tractor**, was creating clouds of black dust.

Bill and Vera Cleaver, Where the Lilies Bloom

BASIC PARAGRAPH

1. Martha went to the attic, ^ , for her mother's high school scrapbook. 2. She finally found it in a trunk. 3. She searched its contents and found a picture of her mother and father, ^ . 4. The picture of her parents brought back memories, ^ . 5. Other things in the yearbook also brought back memories.

NUGGETS FOR WRITING

Directions: Choose A FAVORITE PERSON or A WONDERFUL DISCOVERY or A GOOD MEAL to create a five-sentence paragraph with a variety of **delayed adjectives**. Underline each delayed adjective.

- ✓ Read the sample paragraph below.
- ✓ Revise your paragraph so well it could be published.
- ✓ Give your paragraph a creative title understandable only after reading.

SAMPLE PARAGRAPH for A FAVORITE PERSON

"SURROGATE DAUGHTER"

1. I always admired my mother's friend Deedee, <u>sophisticated</u>, <u>smart</u>, <u>warm</u>, a trio of winning traits. 2. A caring and kind mother, Deedee raised four sons, <u>alone</u>. 3. With only sons, Deedee was on the lookout for a surrogate daughter, <u>hopeful for some younger interested girl</u>, and I was that girl. 4. I loved her company, <u>eager to soak up all I could</u>. 5. Although we were very different ages, Deedee and I, because we had similar personalities, values, and interests, were a match, <u>complimentary</u>, <u>comfortable</u>, and <u>life-long</u>.

OPENING ADVERB

All adverbs tell how something is or was done—*silently, unthinkingly, loudly, softly,* etc. Most adverbs end in *-ly*. An opening adverb begins a sentence. A comma follows an opening adverb.

Single Opening Adverbs

a. **Unsteadily**, she limped across the room and sat in her chair by the window.

Coerr, Sadako and the Thousand Paper Cranes

b. **Suddenly**, all eyes turned from the fire and riveted themselves upon him.

Mildred D. Taylor, Roll of Thunder, Hear My Cry

c. **Slyly**, I tried to check my teammates for any sign that they recognized the wrongness of the movement.

Pat Conroy, My Losing Season

Multiple Opening Adverbs

d. **Quickly** and **quietly**, over the guard's head, George walked away.

Hans Augusto Rey, Curious George

e. **Suddenly, mercifully**, an idea occurred to her.

Stephen King, Needful Things

f. **Instantly, obediently,** Jonas had dropped his bike on its side on the path behind his family's dwelling.

Lois Lowry, The Giver

ACTIVITY 1–UNSCRAMBLING

<u>Directions</u>: Unscramble the sentence parts to imitate the model.

<u>Models</u>:

1. <u>Model</u>: **Gently,** like a mother with a little child, she led the heartbroken old man out of the watchers' line of vision, out of the circle of lamplight.

    F. R. Buckley, "Gold-Mounted Guns"

    a. like a criminal with a conscience
    b. of the teacher
    c. Cranston turned his head away from the stare
    d. **Slowly**
    e. away from the laughter of the students

2. <u>Model</u>: **Presently,** sitting here in the sun, watching the flashing stream, he found himself blocking out the sounds and smells of the street behind him.

    Hal Borland, When the Legends Die

    a. moving her freezing feet
    b. she found herself wondering about the toes and flesh
    c. **Suddenly**
    d. of the feet underneath her
    e. waiting there for the bus

3. <u>Model</u>: **Slowly, slowly** the night came in to fill the room, swallowing the pillars and both of them, like a dark wine poured to the ceiling.

    Ray Bradbury, The Martian Chronicles

    a. touching the trees and all of the terrain
    b. applied to a wound

- 46 -

    c. like a healing balm
    d. the sun rose to light the sky
    e. **Quietly**, **quietly**

ACTIVITY 2–IMITATING

<u>Directions</u>: The model and the sample imitation are built with similar sentence parts. Write an imitation, one sentence part at a time, about something you know, something you've experienced, or something you've seen in the media.

1. <u>Model</u>: **Hurriedly**, she began to set the table.

   Toni Morrison, Song of Solomon

   <u>Sample Imitation</u>: **Hesitantly**, Amanda started to examine her wound.

2. <u>Model</u>: **Swiftly**, the snow kept falling, drifting along the sides of houses, filling the roads.

   Kim Edwards, The Memory Keeper's Daughter

   <u>Sample Imitation</u>: **Quietly**, the children were sleeping, dreaming of the days of summer, smelling the ocean.

3. **Slowly**, **noiselessly**, I turned in that direction.

   Suzanne Collins, The Hunger Games (adapted)

   <u>Sample Imitation</u>: **Gracefully**, **smoothly**, Felicia danced around the ballroom.

ACTIVITY 3–EXPANDING

<u>Directions</u>: Study the examples of opening adverbs, and then in the basic paragraph add opening adverbs at the carets (^).

Examples of Opening Adverbs

1. <u>single</u>: **Curiously**, in summer and winter maggots are uncommon in dumpsters.

Lars Eighner, "On Dumpster Diving"

2. <u>multiple</u>: **Slowly, methodically, miserably**, she ate the jellied bread.

Toni Morrison, *Beloved*

BASIC PARAGRAPH

1. ^, the rain one day in late March fell from the gray sky. 2. It was gentle and quiet. 3. ^, ^, it made the morning misty. 4. It gave the spring bulbs much needed water. 5. ^ and ^ , the rain washed the morning.

NUGGETS FOR WRITING

<u>Directions</u>: Choose A DREAM or THE WEATHER or A SUCCESS to create a five-sentence paragraph with a variety of **opening adverbs**. Underline each opening adverb.

✓ Read the sample paragraph below.
✓ Revise your paragraph so well it could be published.
✓ Give your paragraph a creative title understandable only after reading.

SAMPLE PARAGRAPH for THE WEATHER

"FUN SUBSTITUTE"

1. <u>Softly</u> and <u>quietly</u>, the unpredicted snow had fallen throughout the night, enveloping the morning in white. 2. A substitute elementary school teacher, Jack knew this would upend his assignment that day, but happily so. 3. <u>Excitedly</u>, he donned

boots and a parka, hoping to meet the neighborhood children in their front yard. 4. <u>Carefully</u>, to entice the kids to join him, he began to build a snowman. 5. <u>Joyfully, happily, enthusiastically</u>, the children soon joined and helped him.

DELAYED ADVERB

Effective writers sometimes place adverbs after a verb, delaying them for emphasis. Most adverbs end in *-ly*.

Single Delayed Adverbs

a. The three clouds rose up together, **smoothly**.

Michael Crichton, Prey

b. For a long time, Muley looked at him, **timidly**.

John Steinbeck, The Grapes of Wrath

c. He looked at her then, **closely**.

Toni Morrison, Beloved

Multiple Delayed Adverbs

d. After ten minutes or so we got back in the car and drove out to the main road, **slowly** and **carefully**.

Stephen King, Everything's Eventual

e. When he saw that I was looking at him, he closed his eyes, **sleepily**, **angelically**, then stuck out his tongue.

J. D. Salinger, "For Esmé—with Love and Squalor"

f.   The Devon faculty had never before experienced a student who combined a calm ignorance of the rules with a winning urge to be good, who seemed to love the school, **truly** and **deeply**.

John Knowles, *A Separate Peace*

ACTIVITY 1–EXPANDING

<u>Directions</u>: Below are sentences with the delayed adverbs deleted. At each caret (^) add a delayed adverb that fits the rest of the sentence.

1. For a long time, Muley looked at him, almost ^ .

John Steinbeck, *The Grapes of Wrath*

2. We touched the sheets covering the corpse, ^ , at the edge of the fabric.

Michael Crichton, *Travels*

3. The snake, ^ , very ^ , raised its head until its eyes were on a level with Harry's.

J. K. Rowling, *Harry Potter*

<u>**Originals**</u>: (for the teacher)

1. For a long time, Muley looked at him, almost **timidly**.

2. We touched the sheets covering the corpse, **gingerly**, at the edge of the fabric.

3. The snake, **slowly**, very **slowly**, raised its head until its eyes were on a level with Harry's.

ACTIVITY 2–IMITATING

<u>Directions</u>: The model and the sample imitation are built with similar sentence parts. Write an imitation, one sentence part at a time, about something you know, something you've experienced, or something you've seen in the media.

1. <u>Model</u>: In hunting season, all kinds of small game turn up in dumpsters, some of it, **sadly**, not entirely dead.

   Lars Eighner, "On Dumpster Diving"

   <u>Sample Imitation</u>: On summer beaches, all sorts of body shapes lie down on towels, many of them, **unfortunately**, not particularly attractive.

2. <u>Model</u>: I stopped needing her, **definitively** and **abruptly**.

   Jhumpa Lahiri, *Unaccustomed Earth*

   <u>Sample Imitation</u>: Police started watching him, **secretly** and **frequently**.

3. <u>Model</u>: Some of the younger boys came out on the bridge and began to jump off, **cautiously** and then **exuberantly**, with whoops of fear.

   Marilynne Robinson, *Housekeeping*

   <u>Sample Imitation</u>: Three of the smallest children gathered around the window and started to peer out, **curiously** but then **excitedly**, with eyes of wonder.

ACTIVITY 3—EXPANDING

<u>Directions</u>: Study the examples of delayed adverbs, and then in the basic paragraph add delayed adverbs at the carets (^).

Examples of Delayed Adverbs

1. <u>single</u>: They smiled, **delicately**, like weary children remembering a party.

   John Steinbeck, *Cannery Row*

2. <u>single</u>: As he returned to consciousness, Carson Drew sat up, **groggily**.

   Carolyn Keene, *The Bungalow Mystery*

3. <u>multiple</u>: When he saw that I was looking at him, he closed his eyes, **sleepily**, **angelically**, then stuck out his tongue.

   J. D. Salinger, "For Esmé with Love and Squalor"

BASIC PARAGRAPH

1. Calvin had saved his money, ^ , in a tin can to take his girlfriend to dinner. 2. He counted the money twice, ^ , ^ , to make sure the total was correct. 3. He was disappointed because the money was short of what he needed. 4. He considered his options, ^ . 5. Dinner would have to wait.

NUGGETS FOR WRITING

<u>Directions</u>: Choose AN ACHIEVEMENT or A SURPRISE or A DISAPPOINT-MENT to create a five-sentence paragraph with a variety of **delayed adverbs**. Underline each delayed adverb.

- ✓ Read the sample paragraph below.
- ✓ Revise your paragraph so well it could be published.
- ✓ Give your paragraph a creative title understandable only after reading.

SAMPLE PARAGRAPH for AN ACHIEVEMENT

"ADRENALIN"

1. For the final event, Jane stood on the edge of the diving board, <u>nervously</u>. 2. She remembered her coach talking to her, <u>reassuringly</u>, about the importance of adrenaline, the secret ingredient of championship dives. 3. The water waited, <u>indifferently</u>, its mirror surface unbroken, the audience waiting, <u>tensely</u>. 4. Jane flexed, came off the board, arched, then plunged confidently into the pool. 5. Under water, she smiled, <u>widely</u>, then surfaced to applause.

ABSOLUTE PHRASE

An absolute phrase elaborates the rest of the sentence in which it appears. Absolutes are almost complete sentences. As a test, you can make every absolute a sentence by adding *was* or *were*.

Examples

a. An Arab on a motorcycle, **his long robes flying in the wind**, passed John at such a clip that the spirals of dust from his turnings on the winding road looked like little tornadoes.
<u>Test</u>: His long robes [WERE] flying in the wind.

Elizabeth Yates, "Standing in Another's Shoes"

b. Instinctively, Harry looked at Dumbledore, who smiled faintly, **the firelight glancing off his professor's half-moon spectacles**.
<u>Test</u>: The firelight [WAS] glancing off his professor's half-moon spectacles.

J. K. Rowling, *Harry Potter*

Another way to identify an absolute is that often absolutes begin with these words: *my, his, her, its, our, their* (possessive pronouns). The pronoun can be stated or implied (unspoken).
Stated Possessive Pronoun: She stood in the doorway with her arms folded, **her tortoiseshell glasses propped on top of her head in a purposeful, no-nonsense manner**.

Anne Tyler, *Saint Maybe*

Implied Possessive Pronoun: Then, **[his] stomach down on the bed**, he began to draw.

Paterson, Katherine, *Bridge to Terabithia*

Single Absolute Phrase

a. **His heart beating very fast**, Harry stood listening to the chilly silence.

J. K. Rowling, *Harry Potter*

b. Patrick, **book in hand**, was at another shelf, looking at English soldiers of differing periods.

Lynne Reid Banks, *The Return of the Indian*

c. Boo Radley had been leaning against the wall when I came into the room, **his arms folded across his chest**.

Harper Lee, *To Kill a Mockingbird*

Multiple Absolute Phrases

d. **His feet sinking in the soft nap of the carpet, his hand in one pocket clutching the money**, he felt as if he could squeal or laugh out loud.

Theodore Dreiser, *An American Tragedy*

e. Mr. Barnett, **his face red** and **[his] eyes bulging**, immediately pounced on her.

Mildred D. Taylor, *Roll of Thunder, Hear My Cry*

f. They were walking in the direction of Robbie's apartment now, **the leaves rattling around their feet, a quarter moon flying through the wind-driven clouds overhead.**

Stephen King, *UR*

ACTIVITY 1—UNSCRAMBLING

<u>Directions</u>: Unscramble the sentence parts to imitate the model.

1. On the floor, **his body scarred**, **head resting on one of the man's feet**, lay an old white English bull terrier.

    Sheila Burnford, *The Incredible Journey*

    a. **its fabric disintegrating**
    b. was a rotting yellowed wedding dress
    c. in the attic
    d. **the dress's shoulder dangling from one of the padded hangers**

2. He stood watching the approaching locomotive, **his teeth chattering**, **his lips drawn away from them in a frightened smile**.

    Willa Cather, "Paul's Case"

    a. **her thoughts skittering within there in a messy jumble**
    b. she sat thinking
    c. **her mind busy**
    d. her private thoughts

3. <u>Model</u>: Towards afternoon, **our sacks fat with skinned bark and with tender, torn roots**, we climbed back into the green web of the China tree and spread the food.

    Truman Capote, *The Grass Harp*

    a. we walked out into the cleansing sun
    b. of the early morning
    c. **our stomachs full with scrambled eggs and with fried crispy bacon**
    d. after breakfast
    e. and strolled the park

ACTIVITY 2—IMITATING

<u>Directions</u>: The model and the sample imitation are built with similar sentence parts. Write an imitation, one sentence part at a time, about something you know, something you've experienced, or something you've seen in the media.

1. <u>Model</u>: Dobby, **his eyes wide as headlights,** leaned toward Harry.

    J. K. Rowling, *Harry Potter*

    <u>Sample Imitation</u>: Lars, **his smile bright as sunshine,** gazed at her.

2. <u>Model</u>: I squeezed through sweaty bodies and followed Kenya, **her curls bouncing past her shoulders.**

    Angie Thomas, *The Hate U Give*

    <u>Sample Imitation</u>: Arlene looked at possible choices and chose a convertible, **its top opening up the blue sky.**

3. <u>Model</u>: Sticky watched Dreadlock Man rise into the air with his awful form, **his calves tightening, dreads scattering, eyes poised on the goal.**

    Matt de la Pena, *Ball Don't Lie*

    <u>Sample Imitation</u>: A bystander saw Billy Barrett fall into the ditch with his scooter, **his arms thrashing, legs buckling, bones broken in the accident.**

ACTIVITY 3—EXPANDING

<u>Directions</u>: Study the examples of absolute phrases, and then in the basic paragraph add absolute phrases at the carets (^).

Examples of Absolute Phrases

1. <u>single</u>: James stopped and stared at the speakers, **his face white with horror**.

Roald Dahl, James and the Giant Peach

2. <u>multiple</u>: Charles Wallace in yellow footed pajamas, **his fresh wounds band-aided, his small nose looking puffy and red**, lay on the foot of Meg's big brass bed, **his head pillowed on the shiny black bulk of the dog, Fortinbras**.

Madeleine L'Engle, A Wind in the Door

BASIC PARAGRAPH

1. Leroy stood outside at dusk, ^. 2. The trees, ^ , looked like silhouettes. 3. The air smelled dank because of the recent rain, ^ . 4. He felt guilty about his mistake that cost his team the game. 5. His team, ^ , handled the mistake with kindness.

NUGGETS FOR WRITING

<u>Directions</u>: Choose A CEREMONY or A SURPRISE or A GAME to create a five-sentence paragraph with a variety of **absolute phrases**. Underline each absolute phrase.

- ✓ Read the sample paragraph below.
- ✓ Revise your paragraph so well it could be published.
- ✓ Give your paragraph a creative title understandable only after reading.

SAMPLE PARAGRAPH for A SURPRISE

"CLUELESS"

1. <u>The apartment in complete darkness</u>, <u>all voices hushed in anticipation</u>, the surprise party waited for the arrival of Clarice, there on the pretense that she was going to help her friend put up curtains. 2. The party, the idea of Clarise's romantic suitor, <u>his heart the property of his girlfriend</u>, he hoped might prove his undying love. 3. All her friends had helped with the plan, a conspiracy guaranteeing her distraction, <u>their intentions honorable though misguided</u>. 4. Clueless, <u>her hair a mess</u>, after ringing the bell she opened the door to her friend's apartment. 5. With explosive shouts of "Surprise!" cameras erupted, <u>their flashes startling and upsetting Clarise</u>.

APPOSITIVE PHRASE

An appositive phrase identifies a person, place, or thing named in a sentence. Appositives often begin with the words *a*, *an*, or *the*. They always answer one of these questions:

Who is he? Who is she? Who are they? (**people**)
What is it? (**place or thing**)

Examples

<u>Identifying People</u>: Don Gross was a tough guy, **an ex-Marine who had never lost his military manner**.

Michael Crichton, Prey

<u>Identifying Places</u>: Once they were in her office, **a small room with a large, welcoming fire**, Professor McGonagall motioned to Harry and Hermione to sit down.

J. K. Rowling, Harry Potter

<u>Identifying Things</u>: When it was quite late he murmured something, went to a closet, and drew forth an evil weapon, **a long yellowish tube ending in a bellows and a trigger**.

Ray Bradbury, The Martian Chronicles

Single Appositive Phrase

a. **A balding, smooth-faced man,** he could have been anywhere between forty and sixty.

Harper Lee, *To Kill a Mockingbird*

b. Lou Epstein, **the oldest, shortest, and baldest of the three Epstein brothers,** barely looked up from the cash register when Alfred entered the store.

Robert Lipsyte, *The Contender*

c. In the locker room, I packed for the trip to New Orleans, **the road trip that would change my life and destiny as an athlete forever.**

Pat Conroy, *My Losing Season*

Multiple Appositive Phrases

d. In New York, **the most important state in any Presidential race,** and **a state where politics were particularly sensitive to the views of various nationality and minority groups,** Democrats were joyous and Republicans angry and gloomy.

John F. Kennedy, *Profiles in Courage*

e. The dawn came quickly now, **a wash, a glow, a lightness,** and then **an explosion of fire as the sun arose out of the Gulf.**

John Steinbeck, *The Pearl*

f. Beneath the dragon, under all his limbs and his huge coiled tail, and about him on all sides stretching away across the unseen floors, lay countless piles of precious things, **gold wrought and unwrought, gems** and **jewels,** and **silver red-stained in the ruddy light.**

J. R. R. Tolkien, *The Hobbit*

ACTIVITY 1—COMBINING

Directions: Combine the sentences by inserting the appositive into the first sentence at the caret (^).

1. They were watching a brand-new television, ^ . It was **a welcome-home-for-the-summer present for Dudley**.

   J. K. Rowling, *Harry Potter*

2. His hair, ^ , spilled over his forehead in spikes, hid his ears, inked a few stray strands diagonally across his pale cheeks. His hair was **a perfect glossy black with not so much as a single observable strand of anything lighter**

   Stephen King, *Hearts in Atlantis*

3. On the surface, he was the embodiment of every parent's dream, ^ . He was **a strong, tall, well-dressed and well-mannered boy with talent and striking looks**.

   Khaled Hosseini, *The Kite Runner*

ACTIVITY 2—IMITATING

Directions: The model and the sample imitation are built with similar sentence parts. Write an imitation, one sentence part at a time, about something you know, something you've experienced, or something you've seen in the media.

1. Model: **The only immigrant in my class**, I was put in a special seat in the first row by the window apart from the other children so that Sister Zoe could tutor me without disturbing them.

   Julia Alvarez, "Snow"

   Sample Imitation: **The newest member of the team**, Richardson was trained in a different way from the others in a separate session away from the team so that the coach could help him without calling attention.

2. Model: Argus Filch, **the caretaker**, was loathed by every student in the school.

   J. K. Rowling, *Harry Potter*

   Sample Imitation: Nelson Mandela, **the president**, was respected by every leader in the world.

3. <u>Model</u>: The country hailed Althea Gibson, **the tennis player who was the first black female to win the U.S. Women's Singles.**

Maya Angelou, The Heart of a Woman.

<u>Sample Imitation</u>: The children enjoyed Ronald McDonald, **the colorful clown who was the chosen character to represent the worldwide food chain.**

ACTIVITY 3—EXPANDING

<u>Directions</u>: Study the examples of appositive phrases, and then in the basic paragraph add appositive phrases at the carets (^).

Examples of Appositive Phrases

1. <u>single</u>: Chantilly, **the neighbor girl's cat,** was sunning on the porch steps.

Patricia C. McKissack, "A Million Fish, More or Less"

2. <u>multiple</u>: Maybe their father would bring presents, **a package of colored paper for Ramona, a paperback book for Beezus.**

Beverly Cleary, Ramona and Her Father

BASIC PARAGRAPH

1. Melinda, ^ , was visiting the farm of her childhood. 2. She stood and looked all around at the things she remembered. 3. The house, ^ , was now owned by the Jacksons. 4. The property seemed smaller than she remembered. 5. Only a few animals were there, ^ .

NUGGETS FOR WRITING

<u>Directions</u>: Choose AN OBJECT or A MEAL or A CAR to create a five-sentence paragraph with a variety of **appositive phrases**. Underline each appositive phrase.

- ✓ Read the sample paragraph below.
- ✓ Revise your paragraph so well it could be published.
- ✓ Give your paragraph a creative title understandable only after reading.

SAMPLE PARAGRAPH for A MEAL

"BOND"

1. The family always gathered at the dining room table, <u>a table made by the father's grandfather from a single huge tree on his Carolina property</u>, <u>a valued heirloom</u>. 2. <u>A matriarch with both beauty and brains</u>, the mother now sat at the head of this table in place of her husband, <u>the beloved spouse lost to cancer in the past year</u>. 3. Both children, <u>now a young man and a younger woman</u>, felt the loss as keenly as she did, <u>a widow now</u>, but <u>the new manager of the family business</u>. 4. An empty seat at the other end of the table, <u>a poignant reminder no one needed</u>, <u>a black cloud</u>, threatened to derail the family holiday dinner. 5. Instead, they joined hands, <u>the matriarch, son, and daughter</u>, pulling strength and love from each other, <u>an unbroken family bond</u>.

PARTICIPLE PHRASE

A participle is a word ending in "-*ing*" or "-*ed*" that describes. Participles begin two kinds of participle phrases: present, past.

    Present participles always end in -*ing*. Unlike -*ing* verbs, which cannot be removed from a sentence, participles are removable.

Examples

<u>*Verb* (not removable)</u>: Margarita was **sitting for hours**.

<u>*Present Participle* (removable)</u>: **Sitting for hours**, Margarita would never suspect that some years later she would be there, too.

Oscar Hijuelos, The Fourteen Sisters of Emilio Montez O'Brien

Past participles usually end in -*ed*. Unlike -*ed* verbs, which cannot be removed from a sentence, past participles are removable.

Examples

Verb (not removable): The bats were **wrapped in their brown wings**.

Past Participle (removable): High up under the roof, in the farthest corner of the barn, the bats were hanging upside down, **wrapped in their brown wings**.

Randal Jarrell, "The Bat Poet"

Difference between Present Participles and Gerunds—Like present participles, gerunds are verbals that also end in *-ing*, but it's easy to tell the difference. Present participles are removable; gerunds are not. In each pair of sentences below, the first contains a present participle, and the second a gerund. Only the present participles can be removed.

1a. **participle**: *Feeling so much better after the nap*, Gunster dressed and went out.

1b. **gerund**: *Feeling so much better after the nap* relieved Gunster.

2a. **participle**: Ralston, *going down the staircase backwards*, was very unsteady.

2b. **gerund**: The cause of Ralston's fall was *going down the staircase backwards*.

3a. **participle**: The damaged plane landed poorly, *skidding left and right with sparks flying everywhere*.

3b. **gerund**: The captain during touchdown worried about *skidding left and right with sparks flying everywhere*.

Examples of Participle Phrases

a. <u>*present participles*</u>: He had sailed for two hours, **resting in the stern** and **chewing a bit of the meat from the marlin, trying to rest and to be strong**, when he saw the first of the two sharks. (Contains three.)

Ernest Hemingway, The Old Man and the Sea

b. <u>*past participles*</u>: The master, **throned on high in his splint-bottomed armchair**, was dozing, **lulled by the drowsy hum of study**. (Contains two.)

Mark Twain, The Adventures of Tom Sawyer

c. <u>*present and past participles*</u>: **Leaning against the wall in the hall downstairs near the cloak-stand**, a coffin-lid stood, **covered with cloth of gold, ornamented with gold cords and tassels that had been polished up with metal powder**. [Contains one present participle and two past participles.]

Leo Tolstoy, "The Death of Ivan Ilych"

Single Participle Phrases

a. **Buried in a nearby leather armchair**, Spencer V. Silverthorne, a young buyer for Nuget's department store, slumbered.

Walter Lord, A Night to Remember

b. The crocodile, **pretending to be a harmless log**, glided silently toward her until, without the slightest warning, it intended to snap its powerful jaws over her head.

Rani Manicka, The Rice Mother

c. A woman stood on her back step, arms folded, **waiting eagerly**.

Doris Lessing, "The Summer before Dark"

Multiple Participle Phrases

d. **Clapping** and **stepping in unison**, our group moved away from the swarms, which thrummed deeply and followed.

Michael Crichton, Prey

e. Our father, **dreaming bitterly of Barbados, despised** and **mocked by his neighbors** and **ignored by his sons**, held down his unspeakable factory job, spread his black gospel in bars on the weekend, and drank his rum.

James Baldwin, Tell Me How Long the Train's Been Gone

f. **Filled to the top of its banks, clouded dark brown with silt, belching dirt and stones**, and **carrying blown branches along in its torrent**, it had turned into an ugly, angered river.

Bill and Vera Cleaver, Where the Lilies Bloom

ACTIVITY 1—UNSCRAMBLING

<u>Directions</u>: Unscramble the sentence parts to imitate the model.

1. <u>Model</u>: **Exhausted from rowing**, Grant collapsed back, his chest heaving.

   Michael Crichton, *Jurassic Park*

   a. his face beaming
   b. Derrick stepped forward
   c. **excited by applause**

2. <u>Model</u>: They were together for ten straight hours in the conference room, **guzzling coffee, eating stale bagels, watching the snowfall become a blizzard, plotting the year**.

   John Grisham, *The King of Torts*

   a. on Florida's Captiva Island
   b. **seeing sunsets become a kaleidoscope**
   c. **gathering seashells**
   d. they were vacationing for two April weeks
   e. **savoring the breezes**
   f. **watching sandpiper dances**

3. <u>Model</u>: About a hundred more goblins sat on high stools behind a long counter, **scribbling in large ledgers, weighing coins in brass scales, examining precious stones through eyeglasses**.

   J. K. Rowling, *Harry Potter*

   a. **making sudden changes in direction**
   b. **swimming circles for their defense**
   c. around fifty more fish
   d. swam in small schools through deep waters
   e. **assembling in protective formations**

ACTIVITY 2—IMITATING

Directions: The model and the sample imitation are built with similar sentence parts. Write an imitation, one sentence part at a time, about something you know, something you've experienced, or something you've seen in the media.

1. Model: Rivera was standing in the middle of the boxing ring, his feet flat on the lumpy canvas, **planted like a tree**.

   Robert Lipsyte, *The Contender*

   Sample Imitation: Sonora was looking at the face of the little boy, her face intent on the complete resemblance, **puzzled by the similarity**.

2. Model: In the far corner, the man was still asleep, **snoring slightly on the intaking breath**, his head back against the wall.

   Ernest Hemingway, "The Undefeated"

   Sample Imitation: In the clear sky, the eagle was now flying, **banking somewhat in an upward direction**, its wings open across the clouds.

3. Model: It was the sound of water that Merry heard, **falling into his quiet sleep**, **streaming down gently** and then **spreading irresistibly all round the house**.

   J. R. R. Tolkien, *The Lord of the Rings* (adapted)

   Sample Imitation: It was the scent of lavender that Janine recognized, **happening during her silent reverie**, **floating up silently** and then **spreading completely all over her body**.

ACTIVITY 3—EXPANDING

Directions: Study the examples of participle phrases, and then in the basic paragraph add participle phrases at the carets (^).

Examples of Participle Phrases

1. <u>single</u>: Maurice walked to the front, **winding through the furniture and crates, the boxes and baskets**, to check up on his animals.

   Paula Fox, "Maurice's Room"

2. <u>single</u>: **Warmed by the unicorn's breath**, the boy's fingers began to lose their stiffness, and he managed to untie the first knot.

   Madeleine L'Engle, *A Swiftly Tilting Planet*

3. <u>multiple</u>: Flies buzzed in through the door, **landing on the open water-melons and the sweet corn**, **climbing up the sweating pickle barrel**.

   Robert Lipsyte, *The Contender*

BASIC PARAGRAPH

1. The fireman, ^ , ran toward the burning building where someone was trapped. 2. He wore a helmet and mask for protection. 3. He said a prayer that the person would be okay, ^ . 4. He started fighting the fire, ^. 5. The flames responded, ^ .

NUGGETS FOR WRITING

<u>Directions</u>: Choose A SONG or A SKILL or A DEFEAT to create a five-sentence paragraph with a variety of **participle phrases**. Underline each participle phrase.

- ✓ Read the sample paragraph below.
- ✓ Revise your paragraph so well it could be published.
- ✓ Give your paragraph a creative title understandable only after reading.

SAMPLE PARAGRAPH for A SKILL

"WORD WAY"

1. Clouds drifted across the sky, <u>lulling Monica with their white velvet shapes</u> and <u>calming the jumble of her thoughts</u>. 2. Again she appreciated the sky, <u>wishing she could capture in a painting the shapes and colors like her friend Maureen</u>, an artist working in oils and pastels. 3. <u>Understanding that she could only use words to paint her pictures</u>, she came back to her writing, <u>determined to create beauty in words</u>. 4. Maybe she would begin a book for children, a story about lonely clouds, <u>drifting in search of company in the sky</u>. 5. <u>Excited now</u>, Monica began to write.

PREPOSITIONAL PHRASE

A preposition is the first word in a prepositional phrase. Here are common prepositions: *about, above, across, after, against, along, at, before, behind, below, beyond, by, down, except, from, in, inside, like, near, off, on, outside, over, to, through, under, up, upon, with, within, without.*

Most words that fit in this blank are prepositions: It was _____ the box. (*about* the box, *at* the box, *beyond* the box, *outside* the box, *from* the box, *near* the box, *of* the box, *off* the box, *inside* the box, *outside* the box, etc.) The last word in a prepositional phrase is its object—the word *box* in all those above.

Examples of Prepositional Phrases

single prepositional phrase: **On the whole enormous prairie**, there was no sign that any other human being had ever been there.

Laura Ingalls *Wilder, Little House on the Prairie*

multiple connected prepositional phrases: **Upon the grass of the great plains**, the crooked, bare old thorn trees were scattered. (*Two phrases are connected.*)

Isak Dinesen, *Out of Africa*

multiple disconnected prepositional phrases: **Behind a billboard**, he opened the purse and saw a pile **of silver and copper coins**. (*Two phrases are not connected.*)

Charles Spencer Chaplin, *My Autobiography*

Examples of Prepositional Phrases

Note: Preposition is underlined <u>once</u>; its object, <u>twice</u>.

a. <u>**On**</u> the far <u>**side**</u> <u>**of**</u> the camping <u>**ground**</u>, just where the trees began, they saw the Lion slowly walking away <u>**from**</u> <u>**them**</u> <u>**into**</u> the <u>**woods**</u>.

C. S. Lewis, *The Lion, the Witch and the Wardrobe*

b. The class buildings, <u>**with**</u> their <u>**backs**</u> <u>**against**</u> the forest <u>**wall**</u>, formed a semicircle facing a small one-room church <u>**at**</u> the opposite <u>**end**</u> <u>**of**</u> the <u>**compound**</u>.

Mildred D. Taylor, *Roll of Thunder, Hear My Cry*

c. Except <u>**for**</u> <u>**church**</u> <u>**on**</u> <u>**Sundays**</u> or <u>**for**</u> a rare <u>**outing**</u>, she spent most <u>**of**</u> her <u>**days**</u> alone listening <u>**to**</u> her little Philco <u>**radio**</u> and had learned to sing just about every song she heard. (*Contains one connected, two single prepositional phrases*)

Fannie Flagg, *Standing in the Rainbow*

d. They tiptoed <u>**from**</u> <u>**room**</u> <u>**to**</u> <u>**room**</u>, afraid to speak <u>**above**</u> a <u>**whisper**</u> and gazing <u>**with**</u> a <u>**kind**</u> <u>**of**</u> <u>**awe**</u> <u>**at**</u> the unbelievable <u>**luxury**</u>, <u>**at**</u> the <u>**beds**</u> <u>**with**</u> their feather <u>**mattresses**</u>, the looking-glasses, the horsehair sofa, the Brussels carpet, the lithograph <u>**of**</u> <u>**Queen Victoria**</u> <u>**over**</u> the drawing-room <u>**mantelpiece**</u>.

George Orwell, *Animal Farm*

e. <u>**To**</u> his <u>**home**</u>, <u>**to**</u> his <u>**comfort**</u>, <u>**to**</u> the <u>**care**</u> <u>**of**</u> their <u>**children**</u>, <u>**to**</u> the <u>**garden**</u> and <u>**to**</u> her <u>**greenhouse**</u>, <u>**to**</u> the local <u>**church**</u>, and <u>**to**</u> her patchwork <u>**quilts**</u>, Margaret had happily given her life.

P. D. James, *A Certain Justice*

f. Janet and the Tiger went racing back, <u>**over**</u> the <u>**country**</u> and <u>**over**</u> the <u>**town**</u>, <u>**across**</u> the <u>**park**</u> and <u>**along**</u> the <u>**street**</u>, and <u>**in**</u> <u>**Janet's**</u> <u>**window**</u>.

Joan Aiken, *A Necklace of Raindrops* (adapted)

ACTIVITY 1–COMBINING

<u>Directions</u>: Combine the sentences by inserting the prepositional phrase(s) into the first sentence at the caret (^).

1. <u>Model</u>: The colors were dry and burnt, ^ . They were **like the colors in pottery**.

    Isak Dinesen, *Out of Africa*

2. <u>Model</u>: ^ , they hit the thick tree trunk. They hit the trunk **with an ear-splitting bang of metal on wood**.

    J. K. Rowling, *Harry Potter*

3. <u>Model</u>: ^ , I came out and found a neighbor's bulldog dead ^ . It happened **on a morning after a big thunderstorm**. The dog was **on the bottom of the swimming pool**.

    Wallace Stegner, *Crossing to Safety*

ACTIVITY 2–IMITATING

<u>Directions</u>: The model and the sample imitation are built with similar sentence parts. Write an imitation, one sentence part at a time, about something you know, something you've experienced, or something you've seen in the media.

1. <u>Model</u>: There, **inside the carton**, was the newborn pig.

    E. B. White, *Charlotte's Web*

    <u>Sample Imitation</u>: Here, **beside the window**, was the flowering orchid.

2. <u>Model</u>: Later, **behind her carefully closed door**, Gilly took out the money **from the bureau**.

    Katherine Paterson, *The Great Gilly Hopkins*

    <u>Sample Imitation</u>: Then, **with her trusted best friend**, Diane tried on a dress **for the prom**.

3. <u>Model</u>: **Like silent, hungry sharks that swim in the darkness of the sea**, the submarines arrived in the middle of the night.

    Theodore Taylor, *The Cay*

Sample Imitation: **Like playful, humming birds that flit about the air in a hurry**, the children romped throughout the sunshine of the day.

ACTIVITY 3—EXPANDING

Directions: Study the examples of prepositional phrases, and then in the basic paragraph add prepositional phrases at the carets (^).

Examples of Prepositional Phrases

1. single: **On silent wings**, the powerful bird swooped down upon the bats. (*Contains one.*)

   Janell Cannon, "Stellaluna"

2. multiple: **In the distance**, Kiser Pease, **on his tractor**, was creating clouds **of black dust**. (*Contains three.*)

   Bill and Vera Cleaver, *Where the Lilies Bloom*

3. multiple: **At day's end**, Bryce returned **with a biscuit for Sarah Ruth and with a ball of twine for Edward**. (*Contains six.*)

   Kate DiCamillo, *The Miraculous Journey of Edward Tulane*

BASIC PARAGRAPH

1. ^ Jackson started the car for his first driving lesson. 2. The instructor ^ sat in the passenger seat. 3. The car was about to enter the busy freeway. 4. ^ Jackson pressed the gas pedal. 5. The car ^ smoothly entered the flow of traffic.

NUGGETS FOR WRITING

<u>Directions</u>: Choose A SECRET or A MEMORY or A CHALLENGE to create a five-sentence paragraph with a variety of **prepositional phrases**. Underline each prepositional phrase.

- ✓ Read the sample paragraph below.
- ✓ Revise your paragraph so well it could be published.
- ✓ Give your paragraph a creative title understandable only after reading.

SAMPLE PARAGRAPH for A MEMORY

"REVIEW"

1. <u>In her comfortable bed</u>, <u>under Granny's quilt</u>, Darlene reviewed her day, dwelling only <u>on the good parts</u>, as Granny always advised. 2. <u>On the chalkboard at school in Mrs. Rochester's language arts class</u>, she remembered the sentence she wrote <u>about her best friend Felicia</u> and Mrs. Rochester's praise <u>for her sentence</u>. 3. <u>At lunch</u>, <u>beside Felicia</u>, Darlene's face <u>in a smile</u>, she recalled giggling <u>with Felicia</u> <u>about the bunny-hop</u> <u>in gym class</u>. 4. <u>Similar to counting sheep</u>, these happy thoughts lulled her, quietly, peacefully and finally <u>into sleep</u>. 5. Opening Darlene's bedroom door, <u>without making a sound</u>, Granny, peeking in, smiled.

ADJECTIVE CLAUSE

A clause is a group of words containing a subject and a predicate. There are two kinds: *independent* and *dependent*.

An independent clause relies on nothing else to make sense as a complete sentence.

A dependent clause is a sentence *part*, not a complete sentence by itself. A dependent clause must link to an independent clause for full meaning.

All complete sentences have at least one independent clause—often more—and many sentences have both independent and dependent clauses.

In the sentence below, the one independent clause is underlined, and the three dependent clauses are bolded.

Example

I saw that my old friend, **who had outfoxed Dearie and Ebersole and the Dean of Men, who had gone around and begged his teachers to help him, who had taught me to drink beer by the pitcher and curse in a dozen different intonations,** was crying a little bit.

Stephen King, Hearts in Atlantis

Only the independent clause can be removed from the sentence and still be complete in meaning: *I saw that my old friend was crying a little bit.* The three dependent clauses would be incomplete since they must be linked to the independent clause for their full meaning: *who had outfoxed Dearie and Ebersole and the Dean of Men* and *who had gone around and begged his teachers to help him,* and *who had taught me to drink beer by the pitcher and curse in a dozen different intonations.*

An adjective clause is a dependent clause that describes a person, place, or thing. It usually begins with one of these words: *who, which, whose*. An adjective clause answers these questions:

What did the person, place, or thing do? (*who, which*)
What did the person, place, or thing have? (*whose*)

Examples

<u>*who*</u>: The twins, **who had finished their homework**, were allowed to watch half an hour of TV.

Madeleine L'Engle, *A Wrinkle in Time*

<u>*which*</u>: The man on the loudspeaker began calling everyone over to the track for the first event, **which is the 20-yard dash**.

Toni Cade Bambara, "Raymond's Run"

<u>*whose*</u>: Little Jon, **whose eyes were quicker than most**, should have seen the hole, but all his attention was on the stars.

Alexander Key, *The Forgotten Door*

<u>Restrictive vs. Nonrestrictive Adjective Clauses</u>

A ***restrictive*** adjective clause *identifies* a person, place, or thing:

Example

Already we knew that there was one room in that region above stairs <u>which no one had seen in forty years</u>.

William Faulkner, "A Rose for Emily"

The restrictive adjective clause identifies the specific room. Which room? The one which no one had seen in forty years.

A *nonrestrictive* adjective clause *describes* a person, place, or thing, and is separated from the rest of the sentence with commas:

Example

His black hair, <u>which had been combed wet earlier in the day</u>, was dry now and blowing.

J. D. Salinger, "The Laughing Man"

The nonrestrictive adjective clause describes the black hair; it doesn't identify it. Since there are pauses before and after *which had been combed wet earlier in the day*, two commas are needed.

Note: Adjective clauses are bolded. All are nonrestrictive.

Single Adjective Clauses

1. Mr. McAlester, **who kept the store**, was a good Arkansas man.

Charles Portis, *True Grit*

2. The great coon dog, **whose rhythmic panting came through the porch floor**, came from under the house and began to whine.

William H. Armstrong, *Sounder*

3. He had a permanent case of sun itch, **which he scratched continually without adding anything to his negligible beauty**.

Robert Heinlein, *The Green Hills of Earth*

Multiple Adjective Clauses

4. Lottie disliked Miss Minchin, **who was cross**, and Miss Amelia, **who was foolishly indulgent**, but she rather liked Sara.

Frances Hodgson Burnett, *A Little Princess*

5. She failed to see a shadow, **which followed her like her own shadow, which stopped when she stopped,** and **which started again when she did.**

Gaston Leroux, *The Phantom of the Opera*

6. There are the men of chemistry, **who spray the trees against pests, who sulfur the grapes, who cut out diseases and rots, mildews and sicknesses.**

John Steinbeck, *The Grapes of Wrath*

ACTIVITY 1–UNSCRAMBLING

<u>Directions</u>: Unscramble the sentence parts to imitate the model.

1. <u>Model</u>: All were liberally coated with the luminescent lichen-fungi, **which filled the enormous chamber with a comforting yellow-blue glow.**

Alan Dean Foster, *Splinter of the Mind's Eye*

   a. to the technical explanation
   b. was really attending
   c. **which confused the senior citizens with its intimidating computer jargon**
   d. nobody

2. <u>Model</u>: Betty Raye, **who was used to staying with strangers wherever she went,** seemed resigned to the situation and followed behind them, waiting to be told where to go.

Fannie Flagg, *Standing in the Rainbow*

   a. stayed focused on her problems
   b. hoping to discover what to do
   c. **who was concerned about her decisions whatever they were**
   d. Jannelle Watson
   e. and analyzed them

3. <u>Model</u>: On her monthly visits, dressed in furs, diamonds, and spike heels, **which constantly caught between loose floorboards,** she forced smiles and held her tongue.

Maya Angelou, *The Heart of a Woman*

a. **which sometimes occurred at gatherings**
b. and displayed her kindness
c. prepared for discord, arguments, shouts, and unhappiness
d. at the annual family reunion
e. she tried her best

ACTIVITY 2—IMITATING

<u>Directions</u>: The model and the sample imitation are built with similar sentence parts. Write an imitation, one sentence part at a time, about something you know, something you've experienced, or something you've seen in the media.

1. <u>Model</u>: Suddenly I wasn't thinking of Daisy and Gatsby any more, but of this clean, hard, limited person, **who dealt in universal skepticism**.

    F. Scott Fitzgerald, *The Great Gatsby*

    <u>Sample Imitation</u>: Suddenly she wasn't looking at Mary and Martha very much, but at their accompanying, congenial, handsome brother, **who smiled with perfect teeth**.

2. <u>Model</u>: Sergeant Fales, a big broad-faced man, **who had fought in Panama and during the Gulf War**, felt anger with the pain.

    Mark Bowden, *Black Hawk Down*

    <u>Sample Imitation</u>: Ballerina Tina, a petite Russian-born dancer, **who had performed in London and during the Metropolitan festival**, won awards for her performance.

3. <u>Model</u>: You are now entering Jurassic Park, the lost world of the prehistoric past, a world of mighty creatures long gone from the face of the earth, **which you are privileged to see for the first time**.

    Michael Crichton, *Jurassic Park*

    <u>Sample Imitation</u>: I was often studying history books, the best nonfiction of the twenty-first century, a century of renewed hope for world peace throughout the planet, **which we are hoping to happen within our lives**.

ACTIVITY 3–EXPANDING

<u>Directions</u>: Study the examples of adjective clauses, and then in the basic paragraph add adjective clauses at the carets (^).

Examples of Adjective Clauses

1. The sheep, **which had moved lightly away as he had come into the pasture,** turned now to stare at him.

    Katherine Paterson, *Park's Quest*

2. Slowly I peeled off my black sweater, **which I wear practically all the time,** and stuffed it in my bottom drawer under my bathing suit.

    Emily Neville, *It's Like This, Cat*

3. He pictured his father, **who must have been a shy and quiet boy because he was a shy and quiet man.**

    Lois Lowry, *The Giver*

4. Mr. Posey, **who was close to tears by now,** told the truth.

    Jean Merrill, *The Pushcart War*

BASIC PARAGRAPH

1. Little Weezie, ^ , had a stuffed animal. 2. The animal, ^ , was ragged and a little dirty. 3. The child could reach it quickly every night. 4. It was always on a bedside table, ^ . 5. She would hold it closely in her arms, ^ .

NUGGETS FOR WRITING

<u>Directions</u>: Choose A GAME or A GIFT or A PET to create a five-sentence paragraph with a variety of **adjective clauses**. Underline each adjective clause.

- ✓ Read the sample paragraph below.
- ✓ Revise your paragraph so well it could be published.
- ✓ Give your paragraph a creative title understandable only after reading.

SAMPLE PARAGRAPH for A PET

"NO FERRET"

1. The little boy, <u>who had always been fascinated by all kinds of animals</u>, hoped to start his own collection of pets, all small enough to manage easily. 2. After goldfish and turtles, both disappointingly short-lived, he continued with a kitten, <u>which he knew his mother would like</u>, and planned carefully for his next acquisition, a rabbit, softer than the kitten. 3. Having proved himself more likely to be taken seriously, he now asked for a Havanese puppy, a toy dog named for the Cuban city Havana, <u>which is where this small dog breed originated</u>. 4. For his birthday, he knew he wanted a ferret, <u>which could be the crown jewel of his collection</u>, the most unusual, because no one else had one. 5. Sensitively, his mom, <u>who had supported him in building his pet collection and had helped him conduct funerals for his dead gold fish and turtles</u>, and <u>who had applauded each subsequent addition to his collection</u>, was not in favor of a ferret, which is illegal in some places.

ADVERB CLAUSE

An adverb clause is a dependent clause that provides more information about an independent clause. Like all clauses, it contains a subject and predicate. It answers these questions about an independent clause, and begins with the words (called subordinate conjunctions) in parentheses:

> When does it happen? (*after, as, before, when, while, until*)
> Why does it happen? (*because, since*)
> How does it happen? (*as if*)
> Under what condition does it happen? (*although, if*)

Example

He said the problem began the summer that Dill came to us, **when Dill first gave us the idea of making Boo Radley come out**.

Harper Lee, To Kill a Mockingbird

Adverb clauses and prepositional phrases can begin with the same words. Here's how to tell the difference: if the first word is removed and what remains is a complete sentence, it is an adverb clause; but if the first word is removed and what remains is not a complete sentence, it is a prepositional phrase.

Adverb Clause—Janine, **before she closed the door**, took a look around the room. First word (*before*) removed: *She closed the door.* (sentence)

Prepositional Phrase—Janine, **before closing the door**, took a look around the room. First word (*before*) removed: *closing the door* (not a sentence).

Single Adverb Clauses

1. **While he scrubbed the sidewalk,** I stood there throwing the ball at the apartment building that faced the street.

    Steve Allen, "The Sidewalk"

2. Lesley, **when she felt the lawn mower bearing down on her,** abandoned her half of the wide handle and leaped out of the way.

    Lynne Reid Banks, *One More River*

3. Dicey was up and dressed, washed and fed, and out the door with the day's work outlined in her head, **before anyone else stirred in the silent house**.

    Cynthia Voigt, *Seventeen against the Dealer*

Multiple Adverb Clauses

4. With a gentle forefinger, he stroked the turtle's throat **until the horny-toad relaxed, until its eyes closed** and **until it lay languorous and asleep**.

    John Steinbeck, *The Red Pony*

5. One fall, **before he had regained his full strength,** a young woman came to teach in the island school and, somehow, **although I was never able to understand it fully**, the elegant little schoolmistress fell in love with my large, red-faced, game-legged father, and they were married.

    Katherine Paterson, *Jacob Have I Loved*

6. They waited until night **because nobody could see them at night, because Atticus would be so deep in a book he wouldn't hear the Kingdom coming, because if Boo Radley killed them they'd miss school instead of vacation,** and **because it was easier to see inside a dark house in the dark than in the daytime.**

    Harper Lee, *To Kill a Mockingbird*

ACTIVITY 1–COMBINING

<u>Directions</u>: Combine the sentences by inserting the adverb clause into the first sentence at the caret (^).

1. There is nothing better than a chicken leg ^ . This happens **after you haven't eaten for approximately eighteen-and-a-half hours**.

    Alexie, *The Absolutely True Diary of a Part-Time Indian*

2. ^ , the crippled hound would hobble far down the road to meet him, wag his tail, stand on his hind legs, and paw the boy with his good front paw. The hound did this **when the boy came home after each long trip in search of his father**.

    William H. Armstrong, *Sounder*

3. ^ , Bilbo could see that Gollum was tense as a bowstring. Bilbo could see this **although Gollum was only a black shadow in the gleam of his own eyes**.

    J. R. R. Tolkien, *The Hobbit* (adapted)

ACTIVITY 2–IMITATING

<u>Directions</u>: The model and the sample imitation are built with similar sentence parts. Write an imitation, one sentence part at a time, about something you know, something you've experienced, or something you've seen in the media.

1. <u>Model</u>: She was startled from her half sleep by the sudden sweep of headlights, through the sheer curtains and across the room **as a car pulled up outside**.

    Lois Lowry, *Number the Stars*

    <u>Sample Imitation</u>: She was awakened from her afternoon nap by the piercing sound of sirens, outside the windows and nearing her cabin **after an explosion sounded abruptly nearby**.

2. <u>Model</u>: After rain, or **when snowfalls thaw**, the streets, unnamed, unshaded, unpaved, turn from the thickest dust into the direst mud.

    Truman Capote, *In Cold Blood*

Sample Imitation: Before dinner, or **when parents call**, the children, tousled, disheveled, uninterested, transform from some model kids into the complete opposite.

3. Model: Married at an early age, an unspotted lamb, she had been accepted by a good family of strict Spaniards whose name was old and respected, **although their fortune had been lost long before my birth**.

Judith Ortiz Cofer, Silent Dancing

Sample Imitation: Drafted in an early round, a rookie player, he had been trained with a championship team of expert players whose victories were admired and duplicated, **although their failures had been many before their success**.

ACTIVITY 3—EXPANDING

Directions: Study the examples of adverb clauses, and then in the basic paragraph add adverb clauses at the carets (^).

Examples of Adverb Clauses

1. **While she sat there**, a fuzzy spider paced across the room.

Coerr, Sadako and the Thousand Paper Cranes

2. Lesley, **when she felt the lawn mower bearing down on her**, abandoned her half of the wide handle and leaped out of the way.

Lynne Reid Banks, One More River

3. **Because he was so small**, Stuart was often hard to find around the house.

E. B. White, Stuart Little

BASIC PARAGRAPH

1. Hakim was from Nigeria, where he had learned English in school. 2. ^ , he came to the United States at age ten. 3. He graduated from high school at the head of

his class ^ . 4. His fellow students at graduation gave him a standing ovation ^ .
5. ^ , he felt proud.

NUGGETS FOR WRITING

<u>Directions</u>: Choose SADNESS or HAPPINESS or BOREDOM to create a five-sentence paragraph with a variety of **adverb clauses**. Underline each adverb clause.

- ✓ Read the sample paragraph below.
- ✓ Revise your paragraph so well it could be published.
- ✓ Give your paragraph a creative title understandable only after reading.

SAMPLE PARAGRAPH for HAPPINESS

"INNER LIGHT"

1. <u>When Louise woke up to get ready for work</u>, the sun was shining, its luminous rays penetrating the curtain at her window, making bright lacey images on her wall. 2. She loved the sun <u>because it always lifted her spirit, because it promised a day full of possibilities, because it always felt like Nature's embrace</u>. 3. <u>Since the sun dappled everything it touched</u>, there was no darkness in its path and no darkness in her heart, <u>because she might struggle to find the light on a day of fog and drizzle that grayed everything</u>. 4. Dressed to face the day ahead, Louise admired the light-filled apartment, its space punctuated with sun-catchers on the windowsills. 5. <u>When she went outside to drive to work</u>, her heart swelled with joy, a gift of the sun-sprinkled morning.

"I like to edit my sentences as I write them. I rearrange a sentence many times before moving on to the next one. For me, that editing process feels like a form of play, like a puzzle that needs solving, and it's one of the most satisfying parts of writing."

—Karen Thompson Walker

REVIEWING THE SENTENCE-COMPOSING TOOLS

Below, the same basic sentence is repeated—"*The fire spread throughout the house*"—but each time with a different tool from the sentence-composing toolbox.

Single Tools

1. *multiple subjects*—**The fire** and **billowing smoke** spread throughout the house.

2. *multiple predicates*—The fire **spread throughout the house, climbed the staircase to the second floor, and filled the attic**.

3. *opening adjective*—**Ablaze**, the fire spread throughout the house.

4. *delayed adjective*—The fire, **intense**, spread throughout the house.

5. *opening adverb*—**Quickly**, the fire spread throughout the house.

6. *delayed adverb*—The fire spread throughout the house, **devastatingly**.

7. *absolute phrase*—The fire spread throughout the house, **its walls soon burning and falling heavily to the floor**.

8. *appositive phrase*—The fire spread throughout the house, **an abandoned farmhouse built during the 19th century**.

9. *participle phrase*—**Started by faulty wiring in the old cellar**, the fire spread throughout the house.

10. *prepositional phrase*—**In the pre-dawn hours**, the fire spread throughout the house.

11. *adjective clause*—The fire, **which was worsened by strong winds**, spread throughout the house.

12. *adverb clause*—**After the fireman stopped battling the roaring blaze**, the fire spread throughout the house.

In the paragraphs below, tools are underlined for you to identify. Here is an example.

"DIVIDE AND CONQUER"

1. Ridley, Louie, and Kiwi, nicknamed the Beagle Boys, assembled at the back door, impatient, waiting for Barbara to let them in. 2. In their dishes, the dog food and leftovers from last night's dinner were in plain sight of the threesome. 3. Ridley, the most insistent, began howling. 4. Barbara, John, and Mer went outside, each taking one dog to bring in. 5. Of the same mind, they had learned to divide and conquer.

ANSWERS

1. multiple subject, participle phrase (past), delayed adjective, participle phrase (present)

2. prepositional phrase, multiple subject

3. appositive phrase

4. multiple subject, absolute phrase

5. prepositional phrase

Directions: Identify the tools in the paragraphs below. If you aren't sure, see examples of all tools at the beginning of this review.

"THIN AIR"

1. Responding to the 911 call, Michael, the first responder, scanned the room, noticed the unmade bed, wondered where its occupant had gone. 2. He went to the bed, felt the warmth of the sheets, and knew that he had just missed someone. 3. Perplexed, he wondered where the person had gone, thought about what to do next, searched the other rooms, hoped the occupant was not in trouble and not making trouble. 4. Uncertain about what to do, hoping for a response, he raised his voice and waited for someone to respond and appear. 5. Frustrated by no response, Michael gave up, went outside back to the ambulance, called his dispatcher to explain what happened, and drove off.

"JELLING"

1. Alone, the captain of the volleyball team, looking at a video of their last game, thought about what she hoped for, a win at the finals. 2. Together after many false starts, her team was finally beginning to jell, working as a unit. 3. Intent on strengthening team spirit, they were winning game after game, building confidence as they built skill. 4. Uncertain but hopeful, she envisioned a championship game because they had made it to the play-offs. 5. Resolute in spirit, they could make this victory happen.

"SURROGATE DAUGHTER"

1. I always admired my mother's friend Deedee, sophisticated, smart, warm, a trio of winning traits. 2. A caring and kind mother, Deedee raised four sons, alone. 3. With only sons, Deedee was on the lookout for a surrogate daughter, hopeful for some younger interested girl, and I was that girl. 4. I loved her company, eager to soak up all I could. 5. Although we were very different ages, Deedee, and I,

because we had similar personalities, values, and interests, were a match, <u>complimentary, comfortable, and life-long</u>.

"FUN SUBSTITUTE"

1. <u>Softly and quietly</u>, the unpredicted snow had fallen throughout the night, <u>enveloping the morning in white</u>. 2. <u>A substitute elementary school teacher</u>, Jack knew this would upend his assignment that day, but happily so. 3. <u>Excitedly</u>, he donned boots and a parka, <u>hoping to meet the neighborhood children in their front yard</u>. 4. <u>Carefully</u>, to entice the kids to join him, he began to build a snowman. 5. <u>Joyfully, happily, enthusiastically</u>, the children soon joined and helped him.

"ADRENALIN"

1. <u>For the final event</u>, Jane stood on the edge of the diving board, <u>nervously</u>. 2. <u>In her head</u> she remembered her coach's words, <u>reassuringly</u>, <u>about the importance of adrenalin</u>, <u>which is the secret ingredient of championship dives</u>. 3. The water waited, <u>indifferently</u>, <u>its mirror surface unbroken</u>, <u>the audience tensely quiet in the bleachers</u>, <u>waiting</u>. 4. Jane <u>flexed, came off the board, arched, then plunged confidently into the pool</u>. 5. <u>Under water</u>, she <u>smiled, swam upward, then surfaced to applause</u>.

"CLUELESS"

1. <u>The apartment in complete darkness</u>, <u>all voices hushed in anticipation</u>, the surprise party waited for the arrival of Clarice, <u>coming there on the pretense that she was going to help her friend put up curtains</u>. 2. The party, <u>the idea of Clarise's romantic suitor</u>, <u>his heart the property of his girlfriend</u>, he hoped might prove his undying love. 3. All her friends had helped with the plan, <u>a conspiracy guaranteeing her distraction</u>, <u>their intentions honorable though misguided</u>. 4. <u>Clueless</u>, <u>her hair a mess</u>, after ringing the bell she opened the door to her friend's apartment. 5. <u>With explosive shouts of "Surprise!"</u> cameras erupted, <u>their flashes startling and upsetting Clarise</u>.

"BOND"

1. <u>Traditionally</u>, the family always gathered monthly at the dining room table, <u>a table made by the father's grandfather from a single huge tree on his Carolina property and a valued heirloom</u>. 2. <u>A matriarch with both beauty and brains</u>, the mother now sat at the head of this table in place of her husband, <u>the beloved spouse lost to cancer in the past year</u>. 3. Both children, <u>now a young man and a younger woman</u>, felt the loss as keenly as she did, <u>a widow now but the new manager of the family business</u>. 4. <u>Sadly</u>, an empty seat at the other end of the table, <u>a poignant reminder no one needed and a black cloud</u>, threatened to derail the family holiday dinner. 5. <u>With determination</u> and <u>united by love</u>, they joined hands, the <u>matriarch, son, and daughter</u>, <u>pulling strength and love from each other</u>, <u>an unbroken family bond</u>.

"WORD WAY"

1. Clouds drifted across the sky, <u>lulling Monica with their white velvet shapes</u> and <u>calming the jumble of her thoughts</u>. 2. Again she appreciated the sky, <u>wishing she could capture in a painting its shapes and colors like her friend Maureen</u>, <u>an artist working in oils and pastels</u>. 3. <u>Understanding that she could only use words to paint her pictures</u>, she came back to her writing, <u>determined to create beauty in this other word way</u>. 4. Maybe she would begin a book for children, <u>a story about lonely clouds drifting in search of company in the sky</u>. 5. <u>Excited now</u>, Monica began to write.

"SLEEPY REVIEW"

1. <u>In her comfortable bed</u>, <u>under Granny's quilt</u>, Darlene reviewed her day, <u>dwelling only on the good parts</u>, <u>as Granny always advised</u>. 2. <u>On the chalkboard at school in Mrs. Rochester's language arts class</u>, she remembered the sentence she wrote <u>about her best friend Felicia</u> and Mrs. Rochester's praise <u>for her sentence</u>. 3. <u>At lunch</u>, <u>beside Felicia</u>, <u>Darlene's face in a smile</u>, she recalled giggling with Felicia <u>about the bunny-hop in gym class</u>. 4. <u>Similar to counting sheep</u>, these happy thoughts lulled her, <u>quietly, peacefully and finally</u>, <u>into sleep</u>. 5. <u>Opening Darlene's bedroom door</u>, <u>without making a sound</u>, Granny, <u>peeking in</u>, smiled.

"NO FERRET"

1. The little boy, <u>who had always been fascinated by all kinds of animals</u>, hoped to start his own collection of pets, <u>all small enough to manage easily</u>. 2. <u>After goldfish and turtles</u>, both disappointingly short-lived, he continued with a kitten, <u>which he knew his mother would like</u>, and planned carefully for his next acquisition, <u>a rabbit, softer than the kitten</u>. 3. <u>Having proved himself more likely to be taken seriously</u>, he now asked for a Havanese puppy, <u>a toy dog named for the Cuban city Havana</u>, <u>which is where this small dog breed originated</u>. 4. For his birthday, he knew he wanted a ferret, <u>which could be the crown jewel of his collection</u>, <u>the most unusual</u>, <u>because no one else had one</u>. 5. <u>Sensitively</u>, his mom, <u>who had supported him in building his pet collection and had helped him conduct funerals for his dead gold fish and turtles</u>, and <u>who had applauded each subsequent addition to his collection</u>, was not in favor of a ferret, <u>which is illegal in some places</u>.

"INNER LIGHT"

1. <u>When Louise woke up to get ready for work</u>, the sun was shining, <u>its luminous rays penetrating the curtain at her window</u>, <u>making bright lacey images on her wall</u>. 2. She loved the sun <u>because it always lifted her spirit</u>, <u>because it promised a day full of possibilities</u>, <u>because it always felt like Nature's embrace</u>. 3. <u>Since the sun dappled everything it touched</u>, there was no darkness in its path and no darkness in her heart <u>because she might struggle to find the light on a day of fog and drizzle that grayed everything</u>. 4. <u>Dressed to face the day ahead</u>, Louise admired the light-filled apartment, <u>its space punctuated with sun-catchers on the windowsills</u>. 5. <u>When she went outside to drive to work</u>, her heart swelled with joy, <u>a gift of the sun-sprinkled morning</u>.

FINAL REVIEW OF THE
SENTENCE-COMPOSING TOOLBOX

B A S I C S
   subject
   predicate

W O R D S
   opening adjective
   delayed adjective
   opening adverb
   delayed adverb

P H R A S E S
   absolute phrase
   appositive phrase
   participle phrase
   prepositional phrase

C L A U S E S
   adjective clause
   adverb clause

<u>Directions</u>: Do three things.

(1) First, name the bolded tool in the author's sentence. If you aren't sure, go back and review the tools.
(2) Next, after seeing how the sample imitation is built like the model, write your own imitation of the model.
(3) Then, *without imitating*, write an original sentence including the tool.

---

1. <u>Model</u>: **Barefoot**, Nancy scampered down the stairs.

    Truman Capote, *In Cold Blood*

    <u>Sample Imitation</u>: **Loose,** / the door / swung in the wind.

2. <u>Model</u>: If the contestant, **dizzy**, **breathless**, heart doing fantastic rubber acrobatics in his chest, missed the question, fifty dollars was deducted from his winnings.

    Stephen King, *The Running Man*

- 101 -

Sample Imitation: If the player, **inexperienced, nervous,** fear showing bloodshot red veins in his eyes, dropped the ball, ten demerits were counted against him.

3. Model: As they passed under a streetlight, Atticus reached out and massaged Jem's hair, **a single gesture of affection**.

Harper Lee, *To Kill a Mockingbird*

Sample Imitation: When Jud saw through the joke, Alfonso came over and gave a high-five, **the sure sign of friendship**.

4. Model: His skin, **which is stretched across his bones like a drumhead,** is not white, but a nasty yellow.

Gaston Leroux, *The Phantom of the Opera*

Sample Imitation: Her smile, **which is frozen across her face like a statue,** is not real, but a deceiving mask.

5. Model: Dobby, **his eyes wide as headlights,** leaned toward Harry.

J. K. Rowling, *Harry Potter*

Sample Imitation: Lars, **his smile bright as sunshine,** gazed at her.

6. Model: **Quickly,** they flung a rope with a hook towards him.

J. R. R. Tolkien, *The Hobbit*

Sample Imitation: **Abruptly,** the boss canceled the meeting with a memo to everyone.

7. Model: Toshiko Sasaki, the East Asia Tin Works clerk, **who was not related to Dr. Sasaki,** got up at three o'clock in the morning on the day the bomb fell.

John Hersey, *Hiroshima*

Sample Imitation: Brooks Powell, an outstanding 8th grade student, **who was brother to Louise Powell,** worked hard on his speech for the final assembly of the school year.

8. Model: **Under the begging,** and **under the cringing,** a hopeless anger began to smolder.

John Steinbeck, *The Grapes of Wrath*

Sample Imitation: **After the meeting** but **before the decision,** a clear problem started to emerge.

9. Model: **Immune to the assorted nauseas of space travel**, Scott moved to take her place at the crystal viewport.

Lois McMaster Bujold, *Falling Free*

Sample Imitation: **Curious about the various colors of oil paint**, Sandra wanted to paint the way to her artistic best.

10. Model: A moment later, Pepe heard the sound, **the faint far crash of horse's hoofs on gravel**.

John Steinbeck, "Flight"

Sample Imitation: A week ago, Christina relived the trauma, **the sudden thud of the deer's body against her car**.

11. Model: He was clambering, heavily, among the creepers and broken trunks **when a bird, a vision of red and yellow, flashed upwards with a witch-like cry**.

William Golding, *Lord of the Flies*

Sample Imitation: He was rummaging, frantically, through the trash and discarded magazines **while a companion, a partner in rags and castoffs, worked nearby with a dog-like determination**.

12. Model: I came upon a sight that made my knees buckle, **my breath freezing as I fell to the familiar body**.

Amelia Atwater-Rhodes, *Hawksong*

Sample Imitation: Sammy crept into the room that made his heart pound, **his fear mounting as he opened up the old closet**.

13. Model: Then the face appeared before her, **floating in the darkness, a horrible face out of a nightmare**.

Stephen King, *The Dead Zone*

Sample Imitation Now the memory returned to him, **awakening in the night, a sudden flashback to the accident**.

14. Model: He would stand for hours at the prow, **hypnotized by something out there or held in some thought**.

Michael Ondaatje, *The Cat's Table*

Sample Imitation: Marybelle could garden for long in the spring, **soothed by flowers within beds and tended with loving care**.

15. <u>Model</u>: The snake **took one look at all of us, turned around**, and **wriggled away toward the hills**.

Michael Crichton, *Travels*

<u>Sample Imitation</u>: The child **heard one shout from all of them, looked anxiously, and ran quickly to his parents**.

16. <u>Model</u>: Kit could see the little wooden doll, **bobbing helplessly in the water**.

Elizabeth George Speare, *The Witch of Blackbird Pond*

<u>Sample Imitation</u>: Sam did hear the cheering stadium audience, **reverberating loudly through the speakers**.

17. <u>Model</u>: Gripping the doorposts **on both sides**, Tim slowly lowered himself down, **through the narrowed angled opening of the door**.

Michael Crichton, *Jurassic Park*

<u>Sample Imitation</u>: Watching the kites **over the beach**, Nate carefully moved himself around, **to the soft warm sand of the shore**.

18. <u>Model</u>: **The great square jaws and head, his muscular neck and broad chest** showed his bulldog blood.

William Armstrong, *Sounder*

<u>Sample Imitation</u>: **A large mole and scar, a bald head and bushy eyebrows** matched the criminal's profile.

19. <u>Model</u>: I stopped needing her, **definitively** and **abruptly**.

Jhumpa Lahiri, *Unaccustomed Earth*

<u>Sample Imitation</u>: Police started watching him, **secretly** and **frequently**.

20. <u>Model</u>: Dobby, **his eyes wide as headlights**, leaned toward Harry.

J. K. Rowling, *Harry Potter*

<u>Sample Imitation</u>: Lars, **his smile bright as sunshine**, gazed at her.

"Give us the tools, and we will finish the job."

—Winston Churchill

TOOL PLACES

A good way to achieve sentence variety is to include tools in mixed places within a sentence. Most tools in the sentence-composing toolbox can occur in these places within a sentence.

- ✓ **opener**—tool at the opening followed by a comma
- ✓ **split**—tool in the middle with a comma before and after it
- ✓ **closer**—tool at the closing preceded by a comma

<u>Directions</u>: Model sentences below contain tools *to open*, *split*, or *close* a sentence. From each category—openers, splits, closers—select some models to write imitations.

OPENERS

1. <u>Model</u>: **Desperate**, Frodo drew his own sword, and it seemed to him that it flickered red, as if it were a firebrand.

   J. R. R. Tolkien, *The Lord of the Rings*

   <u>Sample Imitation</u>: **Hesitant**, Cranston took the shortest route, and it occurred to him that it seemed wrong, as though it were a detour.

2. <u>Model</u>: **Unsteadily**, she limped across the room and sat in her chair by the window.

   Coerr, *Sadako and the Thousand Paper Cranes*

   <u>Sample Imitation</u>: **Rapidly**, the clouds changed on the horizon and appeared in the distance like cotton.

3. <u>Model</u>: **His heart beating very fast,** Harry stood listening to the chilly silence.

J. K. Rowling, Harry Potter

<u>Sample Imitation</u>: **His voice speaking very slowly,** Alfredo began reading to the little children.

4. <u>Model</u>: **A balding, smooth-faced man,** he could have been anywhere between forty and sixty.

Harper Lee, To Kill a Mockingbird

<u>Sample Imitation</u>: **The missing, radar-absent airplane,** it could have disappeared anywhere between the Atlantic and the Pacific.

5. Model: **Carrying blown branches along in its torrent,** it had turned into an ugly, angered river.

Bill and Vera Cleaver, Where the Lilies Bloom (adapted)

<u>Sample Imitation</u>: **Preparing many applications for his colleges,** Jared had run into a sudden, unexpected problem.

SPLITS

6. <u>Model</u>: A man in furs, **his face hardly visible in the deep hood of his garment,** stood in the foreground with his hand raised as if in greeting.

Philip Pullman, The Golden Compass

<u>Sample Imitation</u>: A dog with burrs, **its body clearly emaciated with its ribs showing,** appeared near the river with its legs limping as though in pain.

7. <u>Model</u>: Lou Epstein, **the oldest, shortest, and baldest of the three Epstein brothers,** barely looked up from the cash register when Alfred entered the store.

Robert Lipsyte, The Contender

<u>Sample Imitation</u>: Sammy Gomez, **the littlest, neatest, and smartest of the first grade class,** always stood up from his little desk when his teacher asked a question.

8. <u>Model</u>: The crocodile, **pretending to be a harmless log**, glided silently toward her.

    Rani Manicka, *The Rice Mother* (adapted)

    <u>Sample Imitation</u>: The subway, **appearing to be a silver tube**, moved quickly underneath town.

9. <u>Model</u>: Charles Wallace, **who even as an infant had seldom cried**, was near tears.

    Madeleine L'Engle, *A Wrinkle in Time*

    <u>Sample Imitation</u>: Daniel Draper, **who even as a child was always serious**, was almost laughing.

10. <u>Model</u>: Mrs. Rachel, **before she closed the door**, took mental note of everything that was on that table.

    L. M. Montgomery, *Anne of Green Gables*

    <u>Sample Imitation</u>: The driver, **when he felt the need**, made several stops at resting places that were along his route.

CLOSERS

11. <u>Model</u>: James began to sob, **his shoulders heaving**.

    Robert Lipsyte, *The Contender*

    <u>Sample Imitation</u>: The dog started to bark, **its sound annoying**.

12. <u>Model</u>: Don Gross was a tough guy, **an ex-Marine who had never lost his military manner**.

    Michael Crichton, *Prey*

    <u>Sample Imitation</u>: Jenkins High was a good school, **a place which had always suited its student body**.

13. <u>Model</u>: He had sailed for two hours, **chewing a bit of the meat from the marlin**.

    Ernest Hemingway, *The Old Man and the Sea*

    <u>Sample Imitation</u>: Darnell had practiced for the entire afternoon, **playing a lot of the chords from the song**.

14. <u>Model</u>: The snow changed over to sleet, **which ticked against the fallen leaves and rocks and dripping branches**.

Keith Donohue, *The Stolen Child* (adapted)

<u>Sample Imitation</u>: The orchestra played to the ending, **which resounded throughout the symphony stage and hall and highest balconies**.

15. <u>Model</u>: Dicey was up and dressed, washed and fed, and out the door **before anyone else stirred in the silent house**.

Cynthia Voigt, *Seventeen against the Dealer*

<u>Sample Imitation</u>: The speech was long but stirring, lively and memorable, and near its ending **as everyone listened with rapt attention**.

COMBOS

Combos are two or more different sentence-composing tools, consecutive or non-consecutive, within the same sentence. You learned places for sentence-composing tools—*openers, splits, closers*. Now practice using combo tools in those places.

1. <u>opener combo</u>—**Scrawny, blue-lipped, the skin around his eyes and the corners of his mouth a dark exploded purple**, he looked like something an archeologist might find in the burial room of a pyramid.

   Stephen King, Bag of Bones

2. <u>split combo</u>—Huston, **a tall spare man, with eyes like little blades**, spoke to his committee.

   John Steinbeck, The Grapes of Wrath

3. <u>closer combo</u>—Seabiscuit's jockey Red Pollard was an elegant young man, **muscled everywhere, with a shock of supernaturally orange hair**.

   Laura Hillenbrand, Seabiscuit (adapted)

4. <u>mixed places</u>—**At midmorning**, the sailors had caught an enormous shark, **which died on deck, thrashing wickedly in its death throes, while no one dared go near enough to club it**. (*Contains one opener and three closers.*)

   Isabel Allende, Daughter of Fortune

OPENER COMBO

Notice after adding opener combos the improvement in detail and style.

1a. I experienced a rare moment of insight.

1b. **For just an instant, listening to the absolute confidence in his voice**, I experienced a rare moment of insight.

Stephenie Meyer, Breaking Dawn

2a. I saw a young dog that looked like Rontu.

2b. **In the summer once, when I was on my way to the place where the sea elephants lived**, I saw a young dog that looked like Rontu.

Scott O'Dell, Island of Blue Dolphins (adapted)

3a. My grandfather must have cut a dashing figure.

3b. **To her, a home economics major fresh out of high school and tired of respectability**, my grandfather must have cut a dashing figure.

Barack Obama, Dreams from My Father

ACTIVITY 1–Unscrambling Sentences with Opener Combos

<u>Directions</u>: Unscramble the sentence parts to make a sentence with an opener combo. The sentence parts are the subject, the predicate, and the opener combo. Use a comma after each opener tool.

Example

a. took a step forward and suddenly the bush behind him seemed to explode

b. rising slowly from his hiding place, his gun still drawn

c. he

<u>Original Sentence</u>: **Rising slowly from his hiding place, his gun still drawn**, he took a step forward and suddenly the bush behind him seemed to explode.

William P. Young, The Shack

1a. was a thin feisty little woman who had been quite a beauty when she was younger

1b. unlike her son Doc, who was easygoing,

1c. Mother Smith

2a. had grown heavy

2b. above the smoke-blackened fortress whose fresh earth was already frost-covered

2c. the clouds and the burial mound

3a. the black shapes

3b. immediately, although everything else remained as before, dim and dark,

3c. became terribly clear

4a. the goings-on

4b. he surveyed through a scrim of cynicism

4c. slumped glumly on Anna's piano bench before the meal, his arms folded, his chin on his chest

5a. realized what was sticking out of her head was a cordless phone

5b. Sully

5c. as she staggered a step forward, her blue eyes still wide, her hands still shaking in the air

Original Sentences:

1. **Unlike her son Doc, who was easygoing,** Mother Smith was a thin feisty little woman who had been quite a beauty when she was younger.
   Fannie Flagg, *Standing in the Rainbow*

2. **Above the smoke-blackened fortress and the burial mound, whose fresh earth was already frost-covered**, the clouds had grown heavy.
   Lloyd Alexander, *The High King*

3. **Immediately, although everything else remained as before, dim and dark**, the black shapes became terribly clear.
   J. R. R. Tolkien, *The Lord of the Rings*

4. **Slumped glumly on Anna's piano bench before the meal, his arms folded, his chin on his chest,** he surveyed through a scrim of cynicism the goings-on.

Anne Tyler, The Amateur Marriage

5. **As she staggered a step forward, her blue eyes still wide, her hands still shaking in the air,** Sully realized what was sticking out of her head was a cordless phone.

Stephen King, Hearts in Atlantis

ACTIVITY 2–Imitating Sentences with Opener Combos

<u>Directions</u>: The model and the sample imitation are built with similar sentence parts. Write an imitation, one sentence part a time, built like the model but about your own topic.

1. <u>Model</u>: **Gasping, his hands raw,** he reached a flat place at the top.

Richard Connell, "The Most Dangerous Game"

<u>Sample Imitation</u>: **Turning, her attention distracted,** Louella noticed a stinkbug on the lamp.

2. <u>Model</u>: **Sitting in the hot still heat, the flies crawling endlessly on him,** Ben felt everything dropping away.

Robb White, Deathwatch

<u>Sample Imitation</u>: **Waiting on the busy subway platform, the crowd milling around him,** Hank felt bodies moving close.

3. <u>Model</u>: **Grave and solicitous, intensely concentrated,** they crossed the porch and descended the other step to the lawn.

Wallace Stegner, Crossing to Safety

<u>Sample Imitation</u>: **Bright and lovely, absolutely stunning,** flowers amazed the tourists and delighted the young children in the garden.

SPLIT COMBO

Notice after adding split combos the improvement in detail and style.

4a. The great white bed almost filled the little shadowy room in which it stood.

4b. The great white bed, **huge as a prairie**, **composed of layer upon solid layer of mattress, blanket, and quilt**, almost filled the little shadowy room in which it stood.

Joan Aiken, "Searching for Summer"

5a. The canoe twisted and shifted in the rushing waters.

5b. The canoe, **stripped of sail and mast**, **without a paddle to guide it in the swift-racing current**, twisted and shifted in the rushing waters.

Armstrong Sperry, *Call It Courage*

6a. His paper made Grant a celebrity overnight.

6b. His paper, **with its report of a herd of ten thousand duck-billed dinosaurs living along the shore of a vast inland sea**, **building communal nests of eggs in the mud**, **raising their infant dinosaurs in the herd**, made Grant a celebrity overnight.

Michael Crichton, *Jurassic Park*

ACTIVITY 3–Unscrambling Sentences with Split Combos

Directions: Unscramble the sentence parts to make a sentence with a split combo. The sentence parts are the subject, the predicate, and the opener combo. Use a comma before and after each split tool.

Example

a. nearly filled the little chapel
b. forty people
c. dressed in black, somber

Original Sentence: Forty people, **dressed in black, somber,** nearly filled the little chapel.

Charles Frazier, Cold Mountain

1a. moving the tip of her tongue over her teeth, which had only recently lost their braces
1b. looked at him affectionately and sadly
1c. Meg

2a. was crowded with peasant carts laden with grains, vegetables, wood, hides, and whatnot
2b. the market
2c. a large open square with wooden houses on two sides, some containing first-floor shops

3a. red, with a blue and green geometrical pattern
3b. the curtains
3c. were drawn, and seemed to reflect their cheerfulness throughout the room

4a. sorted new students into the four Hogwarts houses
4b. every year, this aged old hat
4c. patched, frayed, and dirty

5a. flew up on to her head and in fury clawed her hair
5b. the rooster she wounded with the stick
5c. mortified and angered, vengeful

Original Sentences:

1. Meg, **moving the tip of her tongue over her teeth, which had only recently lost their braces,** looked at him affectionately and sadly.

Madeleine L'Engle, A Wind in the Door

2. The market, **a large open square with wooden houses on two sides, some containing first-floor shops**, was crowded with peasant carts laden with grains, vegetables, wood, hides, and whatnot.

Bernard Malamud, The Fixer

3. The curtains, **red, with a blue and green geometrical pattern**, were drawn, and seemed to reflect their cheerfulness throughout the room.

Madeleine L'Engle, A Wrinkle in Time

4. Every year, this aged old hat, **patched, frayed, and dirty**, sorted new students into the four Hogwarts houses.

J. K. Rowling, Harry Potter

5. The rooster she wounded with the stick, **mortified and angered, vengeful**, flew up on to her head and in fury clawed her hair.

Bill and Vera Cleaver, Where the Lilies Bloom

ACTIVITY 4—Imitating Sentences with Split Combos

<u>Directions</u>: The model and the sample imitation are built with similar sentence parts. Write an imitation, one sentence part a time, built like the model but about your own topic.

1. <u>Model</u>: The canoe, **stripped of sail and mast, without a paddle to guide it in the swift-racing current**, twisted and shifted in the rushing waters.

Armstrong Sperry, Call It Courage

   <u>Sample Imitation</u>: The glass sculpture, **cleaned with water and vinegar, with a stand to hold it on the living room mantel**, shone and sparkled in the sun's rays.

2. <u>Model</u>: Her husband, **the banker, who was a careful, shrewd man**, tried hard to make her happy.

Sherwood Anderson, Winesburg, Ohio

   <u>Sample Imitation</u>: The dog, **a Labrador, which was her loving, protective companion**, walked slowly to keep her company.

3. <u>Model</u>: The great white bed, **huge as a prairie, composed of layer upon solid layer of mattress, blanket, and quilt,** almost filled the little shadowy room in which it stood.

Joan Aiken, "Searching for Summer"

<u>Sample Imitation</u>: The sturdy brick house, **designed by his father, filled with room upon lovely room with light, color, and warmth,** always welcomed the small happy family for which it existed.

4. <u>Model</u>: The superintendent of the jail, **who was standing apart from the rest of us, moodily prodding the gravel with his stick,** raised his head at the sound of the bugle call.

George Orwell, "A Hanging"

<u>Sample Imitation</u>: Her mother at Matilda's graduation, **who had been standing excitedly near the steps of the stage her daughter was exiting, enthusiastically applauding Matilda with a smile,** embraced her daughter for the winning of the honorary award.

CLOSER COMBO

Notice after adding closer combos the improvement in detail and style.

1a. Rivera was standing in the middle of the boxing ring.
1b. Rivera was standing in the middle of the boxing ring, **his feet flat on the lumpy canvas, planted like a tree.**

Robert Lypsyte, The Contender

2a. Barbara found Evelyn's body.
2b. Barbara found Evelyn's body, **lying in bed, face up, green eyes staring vacantly at the ceiling, long tan arms at her sides, red lacquered nails gleaming, blue cotton blanket up to her waist, a copy of *Tale of Two Cities* on the floor.**

Garrison Keiller, Pontoon

3a. They studied Red Caps.

3b. They studied Red Caps, **nasty little goblinlike creatures that lurked wherever there had been bloodshed, in the dungeons of castles and the potholes of deserted battlefields, waiting to bludgeon those who had gotten lost**.

J. K. Rowling, Harry Potter

ACTIVITY 5—Unscrambling Sentences with Closer Combos

<u>Directions</u>: Unscramble the sentence parts to make a sentence with a closer combo. The sentence parts are the subject, the predicate, and the closer combo. Use a comma before each closer tool.

Example

a. his broken leg stretched awkwardly before him, mending one of Jack's harnesses

b. sat on a bench in the barn

c. Papa

<u>Original Sentence</u>: Papa sat on a bench in the barn, **his broken leg stretched awkwardly before him, mending one of Jack's harnesses**.

Mildred D. Taylor, Roll of Thunder, Hear My Cry

1a. toward the village, speechless with horror

1b. flew on and on

1c. the boys

2a. was a pitiful sight,

2b. the three of us in our overcoats and boots, standing among the dead stalks of winter

2c. it

3a. looked very small and vulnerable sitting there alone in the big old-fashioned kitchen

3b. a blond little boy in faded blue pajamas, his feet swinging a good six inches above the floor

3c. Charles Wallace

4a. the ponies,

4b. were scrambling up the beach

4c. on Assateague Beach, that long, sandy island that shelters the tidewater country of Virginia and Maryland

5a. the cream of the school, the lights and leaders of the senior class, with their high I.Q.'s and expensive shoes, pasting each other with snowballs

5b. they all

5c. were there now

Original Sentences:

1. The boys flew on and on, **toward the village, speechless with horror**.

   Mark Twain, *The Adventures of Tom Sawyer*

2. It was a pitiful sight, **the three of us in our overcoats and boots, standing among the dead stalks of winter**.

   Cynthia Rylant, *Missing May*

3. Charles Wallace looked very small and vulnerable sitting there alone in the big old-fashioned kitchen, **a blond little boy in faded blue Dr. Dentons, his feet swinging a good six inches above the floor**.

   Madeleine L'Engle, *A Wrinkle in Time*

4. The ponies were scrambling up the beach, **on Assateague Beach, that long, sandy island that shelters the tidewater country of Virginia and Maryland**.

   Marguerite Henry, *Misty of Chincoteague*

5. They all were there now, **the cream of the school, the lights and leaders of the senior class, with their high I.Q.'s and expensive shoes, pasting each other with snowballs.**

    John Knowles, *A Separate Peace*

ACTIVITY 6–Imitating Sentences with Closer Combos

Directions: The model and the sample imitation are built with similar sentence parts. Write an imitation, one sentence part a time, built like the model but about your own topic.

1. Model: Now I spotted it, **the address in the 200 block, an old, pseudo-modernized office building, tired, outdated, refusing to admit it but unable to hide it.**

    Jack Finney, "Of Missing Persons"

    Sample Imitation: Suddenly we heard it, **the whimpering of the shivering dog, a lost, forlorn mongrel, abandoned, exhausted, hoping to get attention but afraid to cause rejection.**

2. Model: The Palace Hotel at Fort Romper was painted a light blue, **a shade that is on the legs of a kind of heron, causing the bird to declare its position against any background.**

    Stephen Crane, "The Blue Hotel"

    Sample Imitation: The hair on Sylvia's head was dyed a bright red, **a color that appears on the ads for many products, causing them to attract the attention of many buyers.**

3. Model: The man invaded the bull's terrain too deeply, and he was on the bull's horns, **being tossed up in the air, his legs and arms like a doll's, limp and falling.**

    Maia Woiciechowska, *Shadow of a Bull*

    Sample Imitation: The car turned the corner too fast, and it was in an awful accident, **being broad-sided from the left, its windows and doors in a heap, broken and smashed.**

COMBOS IN MIXED PLACES

Notice after adding combos in mixed places the improvement in detail and style.

10a. Harry looked at Dumbledore.

10b. **Instinctively**, Harry looked at Dumbledore, **who smiled faintly, the fire-light glancing off his half-moon spectacles**.

J. K. Rowling, Harry Potter

11a. We huddled around the gas stove in the kitchen.

11b. **For days on end, in the wintertime,** we huddled around the gas stove in the kitchen, **because the landlord gave us no heat**.

James Baldwin, Tell Me How Long the Train's Been Gone

12a. He could see the United 747.

12b. **In the distance, beyond the Cyclone fence**, he could see the United 747, **the size of a child's toy plane, taxiing toward the small terminal which United and Delta shared**.

Stephen King, Insomnia

ACTIVITY 7–Unscrambling Sentences with Combos in Mixed Places

<u>Directions</u>: Unscramble the sentence parts to make a sentence with combos in mixed places. The sentence parts are the subject, the predicate, and combos in mixed places. Use commas to separate tools from the rest of the sentence.

Example

a. cleared
b. the fog
c. suddenly, with shocking speed
d. the particles creating two fully formed columns that now stood directly before us, rising and falling in dark ripples

<u>Original Sentence</u>: **Suddenly, with shocking speed**, the fog cleared, **the particles creating two fully formed columns that now stood directly before us, rising and falling in dark ripples**.

Michael Crichton, Prey

1a. came over to Jelly
1b. a husky young man with a broken nose
1c. the only other person in the room
1d. his hand outstretched

2a. the paintwork untouched by battle, heading south into the German advance
2b. appeared
2c. a column of armored cars
2d. moving against the flow, and now trying to edge round the same corner

3a. hastened along the invisible road
3b. brightened only by the round of the flashlight
3c. quiet, frightened, and wishing just to dump T. J. on his front porch and get back to the safety of our own beds
3d. we

4a. saw Margo standing outside my window
4b. as I turned on my side
4c. I
4d. her face almost pressing against the screen

5a. noticed very soon one little girl
5b. on that first morning, when Sara sat at Miss Munchkin's side, aware that the whole schoolroom was devoting itself to observing her
5c. she
5d. about her own age, who looked at her very hard with a pair of light, rather dull, blue eyes

Original Sentences:

1. The only other person in the room, **a husky young man with a broken nose,** came over to Jelly, **his hand outstretched.**

   Robert Lipsyte, *The Contender*

2. **Moving against the flow, and now trying to edge round the same corner,** was a column of armored cars, **the paintwork untouched by battle, heading south into the German advance.**

   Ian McEwan, *Atonement*

3. **Quiet, frightened, and wishing just to dump T. J. on his front porch and get back to the safety of our own beds,** we hastened along the invisible road, **brightened only by the round of the flashlight.**

   Mildred D. Taylor, *Roll of Thunder, Hear My Cry*

4. **As I turned on my side,** I saw Margo standing outside my window, **her face almost pressing against the screen.**

   John Green, *Paper Towns*

5. **On that first morning, when Sara sat at Miss Munchkin's side, aware that the whole schoolroom was devoting itself to observing her,** she had noticed very soon one little girl, **about her own age, who looked at her very hard with a pair of light, rather dull, blue eyes.**

   Frances Hodgson Burnett, *A Little Princess*

ACTIVITY 8—Imitating Sentences with Combos in Mixed Places

Directions: The model and the sample imitation are built with similar sentence parts. Write an imitation, one sentence part at a time, about something you know, something you've experienced, or something you've seen in the media.

1. Model: **At midmorning,** the sailors caught an enormous shark, **which died on deck, thrashing wickedly in its death throes, while no one dared go near enough to club it.**

   Isabel Allende, *Daughter of Fortune*

Sample Imitation: **During supper**, the tenants heard a loud noise, **which sounded in the cellar, thudding clumsily up the basement steps, while no one dared go close enough to investigate it.**

2. Model: Neville, **his face tear-streaked, clutching his wrist**, hobbled off with Madame Hooch, **who had her arm around him.**

J. K. Rowling, Harry Potter

Sample Imitation: Girrard, **his arm broken, puncturing his skin**, talked with Coach Jackson, **who had some advice for treatment.**

3. Model: **After the tyrannosaur's head crashed against the hood of the Land Cruiser and shattered the windshield**, Tim was knocked flat on the seat, **blinking in the darkness, his mouth warm with blood.**

Michael Crichton, Jurassic Park

Sample Imitation: **When the approaching storm careened up the coast toward the small town and darkened the daylight**, businesses were totally closed in the area, **resulting from the forecast, their doors locked in anticipation.**

This sentence has five words. Here are five more words. Five-word sentences are fine. But several together become monotonous. Listen to what is happening. The writing is getting boring. The sound of it drones. The ear demands some variety.

—Gary Provost, *100 Ways to Improve Your Writing*

PARAGRAPH IMITATING

You practiced imitating single sentences. Now imitate multiple sentences of a paragraph, one sentence at a time, one sentence part at a time. By the way, the model paragraph uses a variety of tools from your sentence-composing toolbox. Can you spot them?

> "A paragraph's existence owes itself to the words
> contained in the sentences within."
>
> —Anthony T. Hincks

From Rebecca Skloot's *The Immortal Life of Henrietta Lacks* the model paragraph describes a photograph of Henrietta, a Baltimore woman who died young from cancer but whose body yielded an incredible medical breakthrough.

Model Paragraph

(1) There's a photo on my wall of a woman I've never met, its left corner torn and patched together with tape. (2) She looks straight into the camera and smiles, hands on hips, dress suit neatly pressed, lips painted deep red. (3) It's the late 1940s, and she hasn't yet reached the age of thirty. (4) Her light brown skin is smooth, her eyes still young and playful, oblivious to the tumor growing inside her, a tumor that would leave her five children motherless and change the future of medicine. (5) No one knows who took that picture, but it's appeared hundreds

of times in magazines and science textbooks, on blogs and laboratory walls. (6) She's simply called HeLa, the code name given to the world's first immortal human cells, which are her cells, cut from her cervix just months before she died.

Rebecca Skloot, The Immortal Life of Henrietta Lacks

Directions: Select a photograph from your phone or elsewhere to describe a friend, relative, or famous person living or dead. Use that photo to imitate the model paragraph. Imitate one sentence at a time, one part at a time. To help, here are the model's sentences broken into sentence parts.

1a. There's a photo on my wall
1b. of a woman I've never met,
1c. its left corner torn and patched together with tape.

2a. She looks straight into the camera and smiles,
2b. hands on hips,
2c. dress suit neatly pressed,
2d. lips painted deep red.

3a. It's the late 1940s,
3b. and she hasn't yet reached the age of thirty.

4a. Her light brown skin is smooth,
4b. her eyes still young and playful,
4c. oblivious to the tumor growing inside her,
4d. a tumor that would leave her five children motherless
4e. and change the future of medicine.

5a. No one knows who took that picture,
5b. but it's appeared hundreds of times
5c. in magazines and science textbooks,
5d. on blogs and laboratory walls.

6a. She's simply called HeLa,

6b. the code name given to the world's first immortal human cells,

6c. which are her cells,

6d. cut from her cervix just months before she died.

SAMPLE PARAGRAPH IMITATIONS

Imitation One

(1) There's a photo in my scrapbook of a soldier I never knew, its outside edges untorn but fading with age. (2) He looks out at me and smiles, uniform shorts sagging around his waist, bare skin completely exposed, body tanned deep brown. (3) It's World War II, and he hasn't yet reached the age of twenty-one. (4) His young unblemished face is handsome, his attitude energetically ambitious and serious, unaware of the marriage that is waiting for him, a marriage that would produce three daughters and impact the world of education. (5) A buddy on the Pacific Island of Saipan took that picture, and it has lasted seventy-some years in the scrapbook where it stays, within a sepia page and a worn book. (6) He is called John, the unremarkable name given to this remarkable family patriarch, who was John's great-grandfather, born in pioneer days when courage and grit mattered.

Imitation Two

(1) There's a picture on my bookcase of the child I once was, the little girl waiting and watching with interest. (2) She looks at the pony beside her and smiles, dimples in her cheeks, gingham shirt freshly ironed, sunshine catching her soft brown hair. (3) It's the early 1950s, and she has not reached the age of eight. (4) Her animated child's face is happy, her heart still young and innocent, ignorant of the future waiting before her, a future that would bring her more happiness and change the lives of students. (5) A professional photographer took the picture, and it almost appeared on the cover of a national riding magazine. (6) She's usually called Margaret, the name given to her by her parents, which was her great-grandmother's name, handed down from her mother's side several generations away.

CONGRATULATIONS! You learned the same tools authors use to build sentences. Now use those tools to build sentences like theirs.

> "When it comes to language, nothing is more satisfying than to write a good sentence."
>
> —Barbara W. Tuchman, winner of the Pulitzer Prize

SENTENCE-COMPOSING TEXTBOOKS

Below are sentence-composing student worktexts published by Heinemann, Portsmouth, NH (heinemann.com). Annotations below are from the publisher's website.

GETTING STARTED SERIES

Struggles with writing don't have to last a lifetime. Not when Don and Jenny Killgallon's *Getting Started Sentence Composing* series is here to help. It's especially helpful to students who find language arts especially difficult or who are encountering the Sentence-Composing method for the first time.

This student worktext introduces the powerful sentence-composing method. Using real sentences by authors as models, it provides practice with the sentence parts, or tools, that research shows skilled writers use to create high-quality, variety-packed writing.

- *Getting Started with Elementary School Sentence Composing*
- *Getting Started with Middle School Sentence Composing*
- *Getting Started with High School Sentence Composing*

SENTENCE COMPOSING SERIES

With the original publication of his sentence composing series, Don Killgallon changed the way thousands of high school English teachers and their students look at language, literature, and writing by focusing on the sentence. In this expanded series, Killgallon presents the same proven methodology but offers all-new writing exercises for middle school, high school, and college students.

Unlike traditional grammar books that emphasize sentence analysis, these worktexts asks students to imitate the sentence styles of professional writers, making the sentence composing process enjoyable and challenging. Killgallon teaches subliminally, nontechnically—the ways real writers compose their sentences, the ways students subsequently intuit within their own writing.

Designed to produce sentence maturity and variety, the worktexts offer extensive practice in four sentence-manipulating techniques: sentence unscrambling, sentence imitating, sentence combining, and sentence expanding.

It's demonstrably true that *Sentence Composing* can work anywhere—in any school, with any student.

- *Sentence Composing for Elementary School*
- *Sentence Composing for Middle School*
- *Sentence Composing for High School*
- *Sentence Composing for College*

GRAMMAR SERIES

Across America, in thousands of classrooms, Don and Jenny Killgallon's sentence-composing method has given students tools to become more proficient, sophisticated writers.

Now the Killgallons present the first-ever grammar book that teaches grammar through sentence composing. This series gives students the chance to absorb and replicate the grammar used in some of the finest novels, including student favorites and curricular standbys.

Students and teachers will quickly discover how powerful the sentence-composing method for learning grammar is—and for raising students' writing abilities to new, exciting levels.

A downloadable teacher's booklet accompanies the student worktext and includes advice, tips, resources, answer keys, and even curricular plans for teachers who are either new to the Killgallon approach or sentence-composing veterans.

- *Grammar for Elementary School: A Sentence-Composing Approach*
- *Grammar for Middle School: A Sentence-Composing Approach*
- *Grammar for High School: A Sentence-Composing Approach*

- *Grammar for College Writing: A Sentence-Composing Approach*

PARAGRAPH SERIES

Following the success of their Sentence-Composing series and their *Grammar: A Sentence-Composing Approach* series, Don and Jenny Killgallon present a new series, *Paragraphs: A Sentence-Composing Approach.*

Through the activities in this worktext, students imitate how their favorite authors build sentences and paragraphs; eliminate common sentence boundary problems—fragments, run-ons, comma splices; learn, practice, and use the tools that foster elaboration in paragraphs.

With recognizable nonfiction authors as their mentors, students learn skills and build confidence as their reading and writing become more meaningful and masterful.

- *Paragraphs for Elementary School: A Sentence-Composing Approach*
- *Paragraphs for Middle School: A Sentence-Composing Approach*
- *Paragraphs for High School: A Sentence-Composing Approach*

NONFICTION SERIES

Don and Jenny Killgallon's sentence-composing method helps students all across America develop into more proficient and sophisticated writers. Now in this powerful worktext series, the Killgallons use their highly effective method to help students become better readers and writers of nonfiction.

Using the activities in the worktext, students learn the meanings of words in the context of nonfiction selections, promoting deep reading skills: learn and apply valuable tools for writing—the identifier, the describer and the elaborator—for variety in sentence structure: imitate the sentence and paragraph structure of mentor authors from a wide variety of short nonfiction pieces.

The Killgallons provide the scaffolding students need to build strong sentences and paragraphs, as well as to interpret challenging nonfiction texts.

- *Nonfiction for Elementary School: A Sentence-Composing Approach*
- *Nonfiction for Middle School: A Sentence-Composing Approach*
- *Nonfiction for High School: A Sentence-Composing Approach*

ABOUT THE KILLGALLONS

The Killgallons are widely recognized as innovators in teaching writing through sentence-level improvement. As co-authors, they have written many textbooks used by teachers within and beyond the United States, all featuring their sentence-composing method.

Don Killgallon, the originator of the sentence-composing method, a graduate of King's College in Wilkes-Barre, Pennsylvania with a B.A. in English, taught English and writing in Maryland high schools and colleges. Serving as a specialist in secondary education, he was loaned to the Maryland Department of Education, where he worked on initiatives for enhanced learning. He holds three master's degrees: M.A. (University of Maryland); M.L.A. (Johns Hopkins University); M.Ed. (Johns Hopkins University).

Jenny Killgallon, Don's wife, a graduate of Towson University in Towson, Maryland with a B.A. in English, taught English and writing in Maryland middle and high schools, public and private, and was loaned to the Maryland Department of Education as a specialist in writing improvement, after which she had an equivalent position for the English Division of Baltimore County Public Schools. Jenny holds an M.L.A. (Johns Hopkins University). She was one of the original fellows of the Maryland Writing Project

The Killgallons wrote 17 sentence-composing textbooks for students, from upper elementary school through college. Their only book for teachers, *Sentence-Composing Teacher's Handbook* is a comprehensive resource for validating, teaching, varying, and assessing the sentence-composing method.

If you would like to learn more about their sentence-composing approach, please visit this website: https://sentencecomposing.com/

Made in the USA
Middletown, DE
01 August 2023

36115686R00077